JEWISH DIVORCE ETHICS

The right way to say goodbye

Rabbi Dr. Reuven P. Bulka

with a Foreword by Lord Jakobovits

৵

IVY LEAGUE PRESS

D0910549

Any inquiries should be addressed to the Publisher, Ivy
League Press, Inc., P.O. Box 1192, Ogdensburg, New York
13669 (TEL. (315) 393–7600; FAX (315) 393–3873).

Cover design by Irving Osterer.

LIBRARY OF CONGRESS CATALOGUE #92–70080
ISBN #0–918921–03–1
FIRST EDITION, JULY, 1992
Printed in the U.S.A.
10 9 8 7 6 5 4 3 2 1

Dedicated to
untold multitude of
Agunot
and other victims of
Get abuse

JEWISH DIVORCE ETHICS
by Rabbi Dr. Reuven P. Bulka

~

TABLE OF CONTENTS

ACKNOWLEDGMENTS

It would have been better if there was no need for a book such as this, a book on the ethics of Jewish divorce. But there is a need, because there is so much Jewish divorce.

I am grateful to Dr. Robert Litman and his dear wife Niki, who recognized the need and undertook to publish this book. From the outset they took a personal interest in the book, and the elegant touches of the book reflect their devotion to it.

Irving Osterer was his usual helpful self, with his insightful and artistic advice.

Manny Singer on the computer is a virtuoso, and his contribution to the finalization of the manuscript is significant.

Hymie Reichstein's eagerness to help and expertise with that help have been of immense value.

Blanche Osterer was essential to the project

from the outset, with her transcription, and continual vigilant application of the corrections.

My dear wife Naomi lent her critical eye and insightful editorship to the work.

Many people took the trouble to read the book before it went to press, and their comments are shared with the readers. I am grateful to them, and to Lord Jakobovits for writing the foreword.

There may be one author of this book, but there are many who helped make it possible. To all of them, I hereby express my abiding appreciation.

Reuven P. Bulka

FOREWORD

The distinguished author of this book, Rabbi Reuven P. Bulka of Ottawa, is equally well known as a prominent rabbi, an expert in psychology, and a voluminous writer and author.

This work on divorce exhibits all three experiences which he brings to bear on his thoughtful analysis and practical guidance of one of the most devastating problems to afflict modern society.

For the Jewish community this is a particularly acute tragedy, since Jewish life and continuity were traditionally founded on stable homes, now alas disappearing on an alarming scale.

Our national origins go back to creative partnerships between our progenitors and to the transmission of their values to succeeding generations. If this breaks down, all other campaigns for the security of Israel, the fight against anti-Semitism and the spread of Jewish culture become relatively meaningless.

This volume should therefore be read with care and interest. In style and presentation, some parts may appeal more to readers in the New World than in the Old. But I am confident that all will find it instructive, absorbing and reflecting a wealth of knowledge and experience.

Lord Jakobovits
President, Conference of European Rabbis

INTRODUCTION

This is a book about Jewish divorce. It will attempt to pinpoint the root causes of divorce, and the alarm signals that should set one thinking about possible dangers in the marital compact. It will endeavor to place a perspective on marriage and divorce, so that couples who are contemplating divorce know the serious ramifications of what they are about to do.

And if divorce should be the inescapable route that a couple *must* take, this book will propose guidelines for how to go about divorcing in the Jewish way, because divorcing properly is a mitzvah. Divorcing is a biblical prescription, a commandment.

This does not mean that the Torah commands us to divorce our spouses. However, it does insist that if a marriage must be terminated, then it should be terminated in a sacred, sanctified, and dignified way, through a biblically mandated process.

The biblically mandated process deals primarily with the legal document, and the transmission of that document.

However, there is more to divorce than just the transmission of a document. There is the matter of division of property, there is the issue of responsibility to children, and there is the often neglected area of responsibility to one's former spouse, among other considerations.

There is a Jewish way in marriage, and there is a Jewish way in divorce; or more precisely, a Jewish divorce ethic.

Since divorce is so much a part of Jewish life, however lamentable that may be, it is folly to neglect this, and to therefore deny couples who are contemplating divorce, the possibility of going about it in a Jewishly responsible manner. This book is therefore a modest start in that direction.

For the purposes of making the book more readable and accessible to a greater public, it is written in popular style, and except for the most essential, avoids citations and references, which would deflect from attention to the text matter itself.

There are some source books and articles listed at the back of the volume, for the reader who may want to further explore some of the issues that have been discussed in the text.

My hope in writing this book is that it will help couples to cope with marital disintegration. My greater hope is that the message of the book will be instrumental in helping to avoid this very disintegration.

Reuven P. Bulka,
Ottawa, Ontario.

Chapter 1
THE MODERN CONTEXT

~

DIVORCE BEFORE MARRIAGE

Marriage is a serious topic, divorce is a serious topic. Each is important enough to merit an entire Talmudic Tractate being named for it: Tractate Kiddushin (betrothals) for marriage, and Tractate Gittin (divorces) for marital disintegration. In life, marriage comes before divorce, but in Talmudic chronology, the Tractate for divorce comes before the Tractate on marriage. Why? Jesters would explain away the difficulty with the retort that we place the cure before the illness. But marriage and divorce are no jesting matter, and such flippant answers betray an insensitivity to the wrenching pain of divorce, and its impact on so many.

We may conjecture that the treatise on divorce was placed first, thus suggesting that the laws of divorce must be studied before mastering the laws of marriage. This is in order to transmit a clear, precise, and sobering view of how the Torah perceives marriage.

By studying the process and implications of exit from marriage, we gain a truer appreciation of the sacred, binding nature of the marital union. The detailed attention that is given to the dissolution of the marriage impresses those contemplating marriage to do all they can to avoid having to face the complexity and trauma of divorce.

IMPACT OF DIVORCE ON MARRIAGE

If it is true, in Talmudic chronology, that divorce comes before marriage, in the contemporary arena divorce follows marriage all too often. The increase in divorce, which threatened to reach epidemic proportions, has leveled off somewhat in the last number of years, but the sobering effects of the increase in divorce are still with us.

Perhaps the most telling impact of the increase in divorce has been its impact on marriage itself. The fear that marriage may end in divorce—and especially in light of the relatively recent predictions that one out of every two marriages contracted in the 1980's would end in divorce—undoubtedly has had an impact on those who married. They must have thought, or had anxieties in the back of their mind, about whether they were destined to be one of the statistics.

This type of an anxiety can feed on itself. The very fear that the marriage may not last can sometimes compromise the couple's capacity to be really intimate with each other, to share highly personal feelings and to reveal their innermost thoughts and ideas. This is because they do not know whether the partnership will last, and they feel reluctant to reveal themselves to people who may eventually become estranged from them.

Unfortunately, this very process of distancing from those whom we should embrace compromises the viability of the marriage, and may in fact lead to the very reality of which one is fearful, namely divorce.

———

DIVORCE AS TRAGEDY

Fear that the marriage may wind up in divorce is definitely a legitimate fear. It is legitimate because a marriage ending in divorce is a tragedy. The question of how to best counter this fear is another matter. Living in anxiety is certainly not the way to overcome this fear. Putting one's best foot forward and giving one's all to the marriage is the best way to counter this fear.

But all too often, as has been pointed out, the marriage does not work out, for whatever reason. Divorce is a tragedy somewhat akin to death, the death of a human relationship. However, unlike death, divorce is often an avoidable tragedy. It is a sad fact of contemporary life that many have chosen not to avoid the trauma of divorce. They have instead opted to extricate themselves from unpleasant

or unfulfilling unions, not to say cruel or painful unions.

The Jewish community has certainly not
escaped from the spate of divorces, although
most studies tend to suggest that whilst divorce
is a plague within the Jewish community, it is
not yet as widespread. That is a small comfort
on the statistical level, and no comfort at all to
the couple who is divorcing, and to the wide
circle of family and friends affected by the
divorce.

Very few are able to exit from marriage
without adverse effects and negative feelings.
Even the initiator of a divorce often wrestles
with a lonely, exposed feeling that is caused by
divorce. Divorce is testimony to a failed marriage. Some may consider it as nothing more
than a failed experiment, but others may
interpret it as a personal failure, or indicative
of personal failings.

~

YESTERDAY AND TODAY

Because of the fact that there are so many post-divorce singles within the Jewish matrix, communal leaders are hesitant to talk publicly about the virtues of marriage and the negative impact of divorce, for fear that they may hurt the feelings of the divorced individuals in the congregation. This silence creates an implicit cycle of acceptability, changing divorce from a personal and communal tragedy to a mere fact of life.

To be precise, divorce is a fact of life; unfortunately so, but a fact of life nevertheless. Jewish law long ago accepted the possibility of divorce in theory, as is evident from the biblical source and the development of the list of claims for the right to a divorce by either the husband or the wife who is short-changed in marriage.

The modern institution of *no fault* divorce was long ago incorporated as a legally justified contingency in Jewish law. Yet divorce as a general rule was rare, although there have been Jewish societies in various places, even generations ago, wherein the divorce rate was quite heavy. As a general rule, the Rabbis went out of their way to preserve marriages, even to an extent that would arouse the ire of many modern marriage counsellors, who would probably not waste their time on many marriages that were saved by the Rabbis of yesteryear.

~

WE OR ME

A radical shift in attitude has unfolded over the past few decades, away from saving marriages and towards saving the individuals within the marriage. For example, the well known consultant for the public, Abigail Van Buren, under her "Dear Abby" column, was asked relatively recently why it is that previously she would counsel couples to do all they can to save their marriages, but now she gives the impression that divorce could be the answer. She responded that it was more important to save people than to save marriages. She went on to explain that sometimes,

7

in an effort to save a marriage not worth saving, people have destroyed themselves and each other.

This response reflects the reality of contemporary times. Individual well-being, the right to self-realization, personal happiness, and contentedness, have become primary values, to the exclusion of perhaps a little bit of pain that may be endured to save a less than exciting marital union.

The self-realization, *me-first*, narcissistic ethic that has spread over the free world has also spilled over into the Jewish community. Rabbis today would be hard pressed in arguing such notions as "the importance of family harmony" or "maintaining the peace," to couples who are not getting along and bent on divorce.

⁓

DIFFERENT PERCEPTIONS

Relatively recent surveys of the population have revealed some telling information, concerning the focus on the self within the husband-wife dialectic.

Within the 21–34 age bracket, 50% of the males and 67% of the females stated they would not marry their spouse again. The survey showed that the older the bracket, the more likely are the spouses to be happy with their choice of mate. It is unclear whether marriage actually improves with time and people change their views, or whether the later age groupings have a better appreciation of life and thus are better marital partners. What is clear is that in the 21–34 age group, marriage is not faring too well.

Maturity is possibly an issue, with the younger married still mired in the narcissistic mode, and thus too interested in the self. The obsession with self may be so severe that no partner can satisfy the need to reinforce the self. A self-centered person is not happy with the less than adequate partner, and in turn is likewise an inadequate partner.

Within the 21–34 age bracket, 69% of the males and 67% of the females claimed they were the first to apologize in their household. The statistics do not add up, since it would mean that 136% of the marital team apologizes first!

But the statistics do tell a powerful message about what is wrong in the marriage, and what is wrong in the personalities of the marital partners. Each one of the spouses thinks he or she is the right one, the better one, the one more likely to make peace overtures, and the other one is not as good. That type of thinking in the marriage, and within life, courts disaster.

Perhaps less importantly, but also revealing, within the 21–34 age group, 90% of the males and 80% of the females felt that the other partner had more closet space. That adds up to a lot of closet. But it also adds up to a lot of trouble, since each one feels that the other has the better deal.

Different perceptions among the couple, based on a self-centered, more powerful desire to please the self, and a nonchalant attitude toward pleasing one's mate, do not bode well for the marriage. Self-realization, if it is not the main reason for marital rupture, is invariably a contributing factor. Too many people, consumed by an obsession with their own selves, are willing to trample even on previously significant others.

―――

REMORSE AND APPRECIATION

There is an eloquent Talmudic statement projecting the traditional attitude to divorce. The statement is that when one divorces one's first mate, even the altar in the holy temple sheds tears (Gittin, 90b). Why the altar, why the tears? The altar was that place in the temple where the Israelites expressed their closeness to God. One who deviated brought an offering, which was to effect atonement and bridge the distance separating the individual from God; distance caused by, or manifested in the deviation. An appreciative person brought an offering expressing gratitude and appreciation to God for God's kindness.

The penitent has the courage to admit being in error, and to take definite steps to correct the error. The appreciative one has the kindness of character to acknowledge a benefit bestowed, and make a tangible gesture showing that appreciation.

These two fundamental emotions, penitence and appreciation, are evoked at the altar. They are at the same time critical ingredients in marriage. Being penitent in marriage speaks of the ability to see that one has erred, either by not having lived up to one's responsibilities, or by having made an explicit mistake of thought, word, or deed, and then having the courage and the desire to correct that situation.

Being appreciative is an essential component of the basic outer-directedness dynamic of marriage. Expressing appreciation to one's spouse, which indicates a sensitivity to the deeds of the significant other in the marriage, binds the relationship with the glue of caring and sensitivity.

Marriages that fail invariably lack the *outer-directedness* and *willingness to adjust* ingredients. The altar, which also thrives on these ingredients, cries when the couple divorces, when the ingredients that the altar itself thrives on are missing in marriage.

~

TEARS, NOT RAGE

But why tears? Why not rage, why not anger, why not screams? The reason is simply because divorce is unfortunate, a situation to lament, but not a reason to condemn. One cries *for* others, but one screams *at* others. The altar commiserates, but it refuses to point an accusing finger. Character flaws may be at the root of the marital disintegration, but who in this world is perfect? Is it not possible that the fact some marriages survive intact is not necessarily an indication of the superiority of the participants in that marriage? The marriage may just be subsisting, or the couple involved may have been blessed with the luck of having made the right choice.

The fact that a marriage survives intact is no proof that the partners in such marriage are of superior character, and the fact that a marriage ends in divorce is not foolproof evidence that the couple involved in that failed marriage is of inferior character. Therefore, rage, anger, and screams, as a general rule, are not a legitimate reaction. Crying, however, is a legitimate reaction, because divorce is tragic, and for a tragedy, one cries. The altar cries.

Using this model, one can at once laud the marriage ideal and lament divorce, at the same time as one refrains from pointing an accusing finger, or condemning anyone who has suffered the pain of divorce.

We shall try to pinpoint the marital sore points without pointing accusing fingers. Hopefully, those reading this book will likewise avoid accusations, and instead focus clearly on the issues, in a positive mindframe.

Chapter 2

DANGER SIGNALS

~

FOCUS ON YOUR MARRIAGE

There are good marriages and bad marriages, better marriages and worse marriages. Ideally, a couple who marries is interested not merely in having its marriage survive; they would very much like for the marriage to thrive. If they do not, then there is something wrong with their outlook and perspective on marriage.

Do marriages thrive? It is hard to say. Many people are hard pressed to think of couples within their immediate circle of friends who are actually thriving in their marriage. Of course, it does not help when one learns that two people who one thought were deliriously in love with each other, have decided to divorce. This destroys one's confidence in the ability to judge others and the nature of their relationship.

But we should not focus too much attention on other couples, and on the almost silly question of whether or not they are happy. This is the type of idle gossip that goes nowhere, and sometimes can be a negative factor in one's own marriage. One will often see another couple who is not as well off, and say — well, at least we are better than they. This may give birth to a complacency which, if entrenched, congeals the marriage in a state of permanent stagnation.

~

THE THRIVING IDEAL

Marriage thrives when the couple applies the basic principle of "Love your neighbor (spouse) as yourself" (Leviticus, 19:18), to each other. In other words, if each of the marital partners, husband and wife, treats the "other half" as if he or she is part of his or her own being, then the marriage is in the thriving category. In such a marital dynamic, your spouse's pain is your pain, your spouse's joy is your joy, your spouse's concerns are your concerns, your spouse's needs become your responsibility. It is almost as natural a reflex as the left hand putting a glove on the right hand when stepping out into the cold.

Realistically, very few marriages actually attain the ideal, the mutuality and empathetic attentiveness that is truly indicative of a oneness within the union. But there is nothing wrong, and much right, with continuing to strive toward that ideal, however elusive it may be.

~

DEMAND OF YOURSELF

However, there is a wrong way and a right way to approach this daunting objective. The wrong way is to demand the empathy, care, and sensitivity from your spouse. The right way is to gain that very empathy by extending it to your spouse.

Very often marriage gets stultified in the Kansas conundrum. In Kansas there is a law on the books which reads as follows: "When two trains come to an intersection, each of them shall come to a full stop, and neither of them shall go until the other one has left."

Couples can get caught in a debilitating debate over who is responsible, who must make the first move. But if a couple is bogged down in this type of drag-down debate, it is indicative of a flawed relationship, aside from it being a no-win situation. Instead of each pointing the finger at the other, and demanding of the other to make the first move, it would be healthier, both for inner growth and marital harmony, for each spouse to point the finger at the self and to say: It is up to me to make the first move; not to watch the other, but to focus on my own responsibilities, and to do my best in that regard. This is what self-transcendence is all about— looking at yourself, understanding your responsibilities, and then living out life in actualizing your responsibility towards others. In marriage, that responsibility is towards the primary other, your partner in life.

~

CONTINUAL NURTURING

Marriage is similar to human growth. Human beings do not grow unless they are fed. The fact that you had breakfast yesterday does not mean that you can go without it today, tomorrow, and the day after. The human being who desires to survive, to thrive, to have the energy to approach life, needs to address the necessities of life on a regular basis.

Marriage is somewhat analogous to an autonomous life. It is the life of a couple, and for it to grow and to develop, it needs to be nourished and nurtured on a regular basis.

The first danger signal in any marriage is when the commitment to nurture the relationship starts to weaken. Obviously, it is almost impossible to maintain the exhilarated feeling of the day of marriage, or even the exciting feeling of the first year together.

───

SEXUAL DISCIPLINE

In Jewish life, we try to avoid the routinization of the marriage through the sexual discipline. The Talmud (Nidah 31a) is quite clear in its insistence that the reason why husband and wife separate during the period of menstruation and seven days beyond, followed by immersion in the *mikvah* waters, is to regularly recreate the freshness of the marriage. It is only normal that after a while, excitement abates. Jewish law does not take marriage for granted. It insists on certain Divinely ordained protocols for marriage enhancement.

This marriage enhancement, however, only works if it is approached in the right manner. Neither of the couple should dare use the period of suspended sexuality to totally withdraw and neglect the other. There are different dimensions in which each marriage functions, including the spiritual, the verbal, and the sexual. In the time when sexual communication is proscribed, verbal communication is ideal. Neither can be accused of using the verbal communication for ulterior motives, namely to get some sexual thrill out of it as entertainment. It is a time when the couple can effectively focus on the serious matters within the marriage; not that this cannot be done during the time of sexual eligibility, only that this is an ideal occasion for such communication.

There is always a danger to the union when the husband and wife drift away from the opportunities to communicate with one another, from reinforcing their relationship through finding out what the other one is thinking, and what are the concerns of the other. True partnership is sharing, and true sharing includes the sharing of one's innermost feelings, even one's innermost secrets. Obviously this will not happen overnight; it is a trust that evolves over the years. But each partner in the marital union should very consciously push forward in this direction, to bind the marriage in an even closer link as the years go by.

~

ATTENTIVENESS TO THE OTHER

When routinization sets in, and routinization is often the step before boredom, this is the time for each member of the marriage relationship to take stock, and to stop the possible attrition of affection, by adopting and embracing strategies for becoming closer. The best way to do this is to set aside sacred time on an ongoing basis, whether it be once a week or once every two weeks, whether it be one hour or two hours; time in which the couple has only each other and spends that time developing the relationship on a more profound level.

Admittedly, there are marriages that exist, or maybe even thrive, without the couple ever having made this type of sacred time commitment. But invariably, these thriving marriages are categorized by a special level of attentiveness to one another that seems to escalate over the years, almost naturally and spontaneously. When this happens, it is truly a Godly blessing. It is when this does not happen that intervention of some sort is of utmost importance, to assure that the marriage does not get thrown off course.

~

FOCUS BEYOND SELF

Usually, a commitment to making the marriage thrive is the best strategy to avoid the marriage collapsing. If one aims only to make the marriage survive, then this is a strategy of low expectations which can sometimes engender even lower results. And, as was mentioned before, but which cannot be overemphasized, when striving towards thriving, the focus should be on what contribution each can make on his own, rather than on what contribution the other should make.

With all the efforts that one may expend to enhance the marriage, there is no guarantee that these efforts will succeed. Sometimes, in spite of one's going out of the way to assure the viability of the marriage, the marriage does not take off, or does not reach the ideal expression that one desires.

There are times in the marital union when

one or both of the partners will wonder whether they are really happy. It is always better to focus attention on whether you are making your partner happy, rather than on whether your partner is making you happy. Also, it is vital to assess whether your partner is happy, content, and at ease in the relationship.

—

INATTENTIVENESS

Anyone with some level of empathy and the ability to sense the feelings of others, can surely ascertain whether one's partner is stifling emotions, or is holding back from sharing concerns or communicating in a meaningful way. Often, the marriage starts to disintegrate when one of the marital partners feels neglected by the other, and is disappointed that the other has not picked up on a hurt, or a sensitive concern, that may be vexing. Or, it could be an off-handed slight, unintended but real, that sets the marriage off course.

Because each of the marital partners means

so much to the other, a little neglect here or there can be devastating. It is for this reason that the Talmud advised, in strongest possible terms, to always be alert to the oppression of one's wife (Baba Mezia, 59a). Hurt comes easily in a marital relationship, since each member of the marital union relies primarily on the other for emotional support and understanding.

What would be of no significance whatsoever in ordinary human interaction can become a serious matter in marriage. Seeing your friend and just casually giving a wave without saying hello, how are you, how is everything, may not be a serious matter. However, the failure to do so with your spouse can be devastating.

Especially devastating can be the act of omission— the simple failure to commiserate with your spouse who has just had a bad day at the office; or the failure to call up when out-of-town on business, to inquire about how everything is at home. It could be a more serious failure to be with a spouse who has just endured the trauma of a spontaneous abortion, or loss of a relative, and to neglect her.

~

NEGLECT A SERIOUS MATTER

Since the wrong that is involved here is not an actual commission of a perverse act, or a despicable deed, but is more the omission of a concern that should have been shown, sometimes the one who has failed to show such a concern does not understand why it is such a serious issue. This sometimes makes matters even worse, since the adversely affected spouse is hurt that there is not even an acknowledgment of wrongdoing.

It is easy for resentments to build up in such a scenario, because there is so much reliance on the partner for emotional support, and great disappointment when that support is not forthcoming. Disappointment is often the prelude to bottled up resentment and ill-feeling that can adversely affect the marriage in all its dimensions.

Human beings are usually quite good at sniffing out what it is that they need, and are also very alert to the hurt that may be inflicted upon them either directly or by neglect. It is when they do this to others that human beings usually lack commensurate alertness. However, the operative dynamic of "Love your neighbor as yourself," seeing your spouse as part of you, is likewise an imperative to be alert to those hurts of your spouse, as if they were your own.

Thus, resentment, suppressed emotions, withdrawal from vibrant communication, a sense of being upset, or down, or even depressed, are indications that something is wrong. It may not necessarily be something that is wrong with the marriage; it may simply be something that is bothering your spouse. But if it bothers your spouse, and you do nothing about it, it can then become an impediment in the marital relationship.

~

AGREEABLE DISAGREEMENT

Ideally, one would like to go through the entire marriage without having any arguments with one's spouse. However, that is a difficult ideal to achieve. One may even argue that having disagreements is not necessarily the end of the world. It is not whether or not husband and wife disagree that is as crucial as the question of how they disagree.

If the disagreement is on issues of importance, and it is carried out with respectfulness for the other one's person and the other one's opinion, then that disagreement can be a healthful exercise. It should result in a consensual agreement based on an appreciation by each of the other's viewpoint. This is one of the singular advantages that comes with marriage; the combining of two viewpoints, the sharing of ideas, and the mutual enhancement that comes from greater input.

When the argument becomes embittered with personal aspersions, when the argument is projected in a heavy-handed manner with lack of respect for the other, then this is a danger signal in the marital dynamics.

It goes without need for elaboration that abuse of one's partner, physical or verbal, is unconscionable, and its manifestation in marriage is a danger signal of the most serious magnitude.

Neither of the spouses has the right to impose views, or to become a dictator in the marital context. Lack of mutuality and consultation, be it on matters of finances, on matters of where to go for a vacation, or where to send the children to school or to camp, or any other issue, are an indication of a fundamental imbalance and deficit in marital communication.

~

RELIGIOUS DISPARITY

Religious differences too can interfere with marital harmony. When the couple is not onside in their religious commitment, when each goes in a different direction, the marital balance is upset. If, for example, the husband or the wife has suddenly decided, for whatever reason, to escalate religious observance, and does so with a great amount of exuberance, there is a danger of leaving the other one behind and creating a schism within the marriage.

This is not to say that one should hold back on developing religiously. It is to say that in becoming more embracing of religious categories, one should also at the same time embrace the religious category of loving one's spouse, and make sure that whatever develops does so in harmony and in partnership. Granted, this is difficult, and arguably even sometimes impossible. It still is nevertheless vital for a spouse who has become more conscious of and sensitive to religious expression, to make sure that religious expression does not become the first step towards marital disintegration.

The Midrash (Leviticus Rabbah, 9:9), in a fascinating vignette, states that to save a marriage, there is even a ritual of erasing the name of God, which under normal circumstances is a most grievous breach. This projects the vital notion that God willingly steps to the sideline in order to save a marriage. The message and the implication are clear. To use God or Godliness as the excuse or cause for driving a wedge in the marriage is a distortion of the Godly.

~

CONJUGAL DIFFICULTIES

Finally, one of the clear danger signals that marriage is not the way it ought to be is the matter of conjugal relations. With this component of marriage, as with others, much depends on the nature of the relationship as it evolves. What may be a danger signal for some couples may be nothing more than the usual for others. All human beings are different, and the nature of how they relate to each other is a unique expression of their differentness.

However, each of the marital partners can know very well through what goes on in the bedroom whether there is something wrong in the marriage.

This is not to suggest that there must be a pressure placed upon either spouse to "perform" as per the societal dictates. What is of utmost concern is not sexual performance; what is of utmost concern is the caring, sensitivity and warmth that should characterize the embracing moment. Technique is not what is at issue; affection is what is at issue. When affection is lacking, or when there is disinterest in the personal communication and more in just the physical thrill, then this is a warning signal that all is not well in the relationship.

Whether or not a conjugal experience is successful is not related to the proper exercise of "technique," as much as to the expression of true affection and the showering of love. This is the primary ingredient in the conjugal union, and of course the primary ingredient in marriage. When this is missing, it is a red alert, a call for action.

Extra-marital involvement is a more serious impediment to the marriage. Most often the extra-marital affair is the result, rather than the cause, of marital difficulty. However, although it is only the result of marital difficulty, it could easily become the cause of marital collapse.

~

ALERT TO DANGERS

This chapter has spelled out some, but not all the danger signals that can impede the marital flow. There are others, such as the financial woes that can disrupt even a smooth relationship. Interference of relatives can also cause problems, as can the ill health, physical or mental, of either spouse, or other members of the family. The loss of a child is also a potential danger point. One of the couple may be mired in melancholy as a result of the loss, whilst the other may want to get on with life. The spouses go in diverging paths, often to the point of divorcing.

Not all danger signals are an indication that the marriage is on the rocks and doomed to failure. They are only to be seen as alarm clock awakenings to the fact that the marriage, even if it is good, is languishing in the problem areas that need to be confronted, for the marriage to continue along the road toward thriving.

If one is oblivious to the dangers, then one risks marital stagnation, and possible marital disintegration. In being alert to the danger signals, one is alert to the responsibility to intervene at the earliest possible moment, to head-off the syndrome that can be generated by the undesirable realities.

Chapter 3

WHAT TO DO WHEN THINGS START GOING WRONG

~

AVOID PROCRASTINATION

When the danger signals as spelled out in the previous chapter start to appear, the worst reaction is to push them off, to trivialize them and say they are unimportant. By so doing, one becomes indifferent. That type of indifference spills over into the entirety of the marital relationship.

Precisely because they are danger signals, precisely because of this must they be taken seriously and acted upon with sensitivity, with genuine concern, and with immediacy. There are a number of steps to take when things start going wrong. What one does when things start going wrong can actually make or break the relationship.

———

THE RIGHT AND WRONG QUESTION

The first thing to do when things start going wrong is to take a sober and serious look at oneself. The natural tendency is to push off all blame on to others, and in marriage the ever-available other is one's spouse. But blaming one's spouse and putting all of the fault for what has gone sour on the other person is almost always unfair, inaccurate, wrong, and destructive. Anyone who sees the self as being the victim of all that has transpired, and far beyond any criticism, is an unlikely candidate for helping to make things better.

Therefore, it is essential, when things start going wrong, to begin with oneself. One should make a detached and objective analysis of one's behavior in the marriage. There are a number of questions that must be asked seriously, and must be answered with honesty and forthrightness. Have I been fair to my spouse? Have I given my spouse the attention that my spouse deserves? Have I lived up to my responsibilities within the marriage? Have I gone out of my way to make my spouse feel loved, appreciated, and respected? Have I shown in tangible ways how much my spouse means to me? Have I taken the time to listen carefully to my spouse's concerns? Have I addressed my spouse's needs?

These are questions that are often asked in marriage, but unfortunately, the way the question is phrased is quite different. Instead of asking: "Have I shown my spouse love, care, and appreciation?" the question asked is: "Has my spouse shown me love, care, and appreciation?"

But that type of question is the wrong question, at least at the very outset. Relationships are often mirror reflections, but demanding that the other do for you before you do for the other ends in a stalemate, and no one wants to be married to a stalemate.

―

COMMITMENT TO TRY

In the process of reflecting on where and how things have gone wrong, it is also useful to look at when things started to go wrong. Was the marriage always tenuous, or were there times when everything seemed to be going quite smoothly? If the marriage was always shaky, then one should go backwards to the time prior to the marriage. Was everything smooth before, during the engagement period or prior to that, or was this entire relationship one that was forced from the beginning, and should never have been finalized?

Obviously, if this is the case, it will be much more difficult to put things back together. For after all, it is very difficult to put back together what was never really together. Still, this does not necessarily preclude the possibility of putting the marriage on track. The fact that it never was good does not mean that it will never be good. With maximal effort, and with each one of the couple doing the utmost to correct what has gone wrong, such mid-course correction is still achievable.

The couple owes it to each other, because of the investment in time and emotional energy each has placed in the other, to give the marriage a fair chance of working out. Not doing so would be a breach of fundamental Judaic ethics, the ethics that emanate from the obligation we have to love our spouse as our own self, and to do for the marital partner what we would want to do for ourselves, namely to assure togetherness and meaningful love. If after all the effort this cannot be achieved, then there is a process for termination. But that termination process should be entered into only after all serious effort to right all that went wrong has been exhausted.

~

EXCITING OR STABLE

In looking backwards at the marriage, the other scenario is that the marriage was exciting and thriving at one point in time, but things have not been the same for a while. Here some significant factors need to be taken into account. Realistically, it is impossible to maintain the excitement of the first week, month, and year of marriage. Over the long haul, marriage stabilizes from excitement to a more permanent and meaningful plateau of respect, love that is founded on respect, and devotion. These may not be exciting words, and they may not even bring excitement to the marriage. But a successful marriage is not one that is always exciting; it is one that is caring, giving, and understanding. It is solid, reliable, and secure.

Excitement is a desirable high, but it is a high that is best achieved coming from a plateau rather than coming from a valley. A marriage which oscillates between the valley of despair and the periodic excitement of ecstatic pleasure is a marriage which is in trouble. Eventually the peak pleasure as the saving grace of the marriage will lose its luster, even as it becomes almost a harbinger of the despair that usually follows.

If the problem in the marriage is one that is related to the failure to maintain the relatively high level of excitement, then this may not be a serious impediment to the relationship. It more likely reflects a need to adjust one's mind-set to the reality of what married life is all about.

~

WHEN DID IT START

However, it is possible for marriage to take a serious downturn, from once having been a very good marriage, to now being a marriage in trouble. It is in this type of situation that each one of the couple is well advised to reflect backwards, to try to pinpoint as precisely as possible exactly when the marriage started to flounder. It could be a specific episode, an event, or even a non-event that triggered this downturn. Very often it is possible that one can pinpoint the moment of downturn in time, without being able to accurately describe the cause for the downturn. For this, one invariably needs the help of one's partner, if not an outside intervener.

The downturn could come after a failed pregnancy, after childbirth, following a traumatic event within the family, such as a child being sick, or a parent passing away. It could involve the feeling of one spouse that the other spouse was not sensitive enough to feelings. Or it could be something as trivial as forgetting an anniversary or birthday. What this may trigger is hard to predict, but quite often it changes a positive-flow relationship into a negative-flow relationship.

In a positive flow, everything moves forward smoothly. Everyone is centered and focused on the marital union in an affirmative, optimistic way. When the marriage gets into a negative-flow situation, then negativity feeds on itself. Even a neutral behavior is looked upon with dark glasses. Each of the spouses, or at least the offended spouse, is more critical of the other, and the relationship begins to fall apart.

~

TAKE FEELINGS SERIOUSLY

Pinpointing when it went wrong, why it went wrong, and how it went wrong, is therefore crucial to the rebuilding process. Admittedly, one can rebuild by forgetting what happened in the past; letting bygones be bygones and starting again. That can work, but it always invites the danger that whatever precipitated the original crisis might recur. It is better to try to find the cause of the problem, in order to avoid its repetition.

Since a marriage that thrives is based on the shared feelings of the couple and the sensitivity of each of the spouses towards the other, it is unwise and counterproductive to make value judgments about those feelings. A husband, in a typical situation, may feel that his wife's sensitivity about not saying nice things to her when she was going through a miscarriage is a trivial matter; that he really cared but that he did not think he needed to show it so overtly.

In the matter of feelings, especially feelings between husband and wife, the key to marital thriving is to know precisely what one's spouse needs, and to provide that need. It may be trivial to the offending party, but it is certainly not trivial to the offended party. This is the crucial concern.

～

COMMUNAL STAKE

Although it is best for mature adults to be able to work out their problems on their own, and to address their difficulties with objectivity and seriousness, it is obvious that often the problem may have become too big for the couple to handle on their own. When this occurs, it is time for the couple to swallow their pride, to realize it is a problem for which they need some form of outside help.

It is wrong to be cavalier about the situation, to say if it takes outside help to save the marriage, then maybe it is not worth saving. Although divorce has become more prevalent, this does not make it more desirable. Stable marriages, solid marriages, marriages based on a firm commitment to see things through until and unless living together is impossible, remain the basis for a vibrant community. The marriage is bigger than the couple involved in the marriage. Although they are the main players, it is the community itself which is at stake. This must be a primary concern and focus as the couple approaches the crisis in their relationship.

To illustrate this point about community, the *seven days* after marriage require an intense closeness between husband and wife, in which neither one can waive that obligation of closeness towards the other. They must be with each other for the entire time.

This is based on the assumption that even though it may not matter to them, the necessity of setting the marriage on a firm footing is so vital to the community interest that neither bride nor groom has the right to waive what is not merely a personal right; it is also a communal concern. That which is totally and solely in one's personal domain one can forego and forgive. But once it becomes bigger than personal and private, the rules change.

Since it is the community that is also of concern in the marital crisis, the couple is urged to do whatever they can, even seeking outside help, to set the marriage back on its proper course.

~

SEEKING HELP

Who should be the outside intervener for the troubled couple? It could be any one of a number of types. It could be a Rabbi whom the couple trusts; one who knows the couple, or who was even involved in their marrying. It could be a Rabbi whom the couple do not know at all, but who has a well-earned reputation for helping couples who are in difficulty. It could be a marriage counsellor, or a psychologist with special expertise in marital problems.

When choosing within the realm of professionals, it is important to select someone with a bias, namely a bias towards marriage. It would be wrong to seek out someone who does not have a commitment to seriously exploring whatever can be done to save the marriage. For marital counselling, seeking out a counsellor who is not committed to helping the marriage to whatever extent possible is the equivalent of seeking out a medical doctor who is not committed to saving life.

~

MAKING HELP WORK

The entry through the therapeutic door, as humbling as it may be, is well worth it, if it is the remedial step that is necessary to save the marriage and make it thrive. Aside from this endeavor being much less traumatic than divorce, it also offers the possibility that one may regain a relationship and avoid loneliness.

Once having made the commitment to therapy, each one of the couple must do so with the uncompromising intention to give one's maximum effort to the process, and to be as cooperative, as open to suggestion and to change as possible, in order to effect some positive momentum.

Going into this endeavor with the attitude that I am only doing it to satisfy myself that I made the effort, or going into it with the attitude that it is the other one who has to do the changing and I am only there to facilitate that, is almost a guarantee that the exercise will fail. Each one of the couple must go in ready to do the changing and the adjusting, rather than demanding it of the other. Only then will the real possibility for improvement be a likely prospect.

———

TALKING TO OTHERS

During the time that the marriage is going through its transitional phase of confronting difficulties, it is useful to be open to other activities that can help. Aside from the possibilities that are opened up via therapy, much can be gained by speaking to friends who have gone through this same trauma, those who either have had difficulties and overcome them, or had difficulties and failed to overcome them. Not every couple that has gone through divorce is happy in retrospect with that fact. More and more one hears of couples who lament the fact that the marriage ended up in divorce, who complain that they received bad advice from people who really had no stake in the marriage; advice which drove a wedge between the spouses, rather than creating the prospects for any reconciliation.

It is important to avoid the lawyer trap that sometimes creates artificial distance and coldness between husband and wife. One should also avoid getting into a me-first type of therapy, wherein individual happiness is so supreme that any form of struggle toward adjustment is deemed inappropriate, and saving of the marriage unnecessary.

~

PROJECTING THE FUTURE

Speaking with people who have been through it all can help. It is also beneficial to explore quite seriously the consequences of the decision to divorce, before it is made. These consequences include the emotional and purely practical domains. Although it is quite difficult to project how one will feel after separation, one can at least try to project what life will be like coming home to an empty apartment, or depending on custodial arrangements; what it would be like to be a single parent.

Too often a couple is so ready to divorce because of present frustrations that they do not care about the consequences that await them. They feel, sometimes rightly, sometimes wrongly, that no matter what, the new situation will be better than the present predicament. But this is not always the case. Sober projection of what awaits the separating spouses, individually and collectively, is of vital necessity before jumping towards divorce.

~

THE FINANCIAL CRUNCH

There are many problems associated with divorce, not the least of which is the reality that with divorce comes a financial crunch. For those couples who are independently wealthy and for whom financial matters are of no concern, the issue is not as crucial. However, for any one in the middle class or below, divorce is potentially devastating financially.

If two can live cheaper than one, then one lives much more expensively than two. Additionally, for the supporting spouse, who now must live singly, there is also an obligation to provide support for the other spouse.

It is usually the husband who must supply this support. The wife who is dependent on this support is certainly in a disadvantaged position. The husband who must supply this support, aside from an extra rent and other personal living expenses, will also be hard-pressed to maintain the living standard that had been the previous status quo. It becomes readily apparent that divorce is not a panacea on a financial level, and very often it is not even a panacea on the emotional level. It is therefore absolutely essential, before rushing to divorce, to know exactly what that decision entails and what it implies for the future.

IMPACT ON CHILDREN

Needless to say, the impact of divorce on children is also of vital concern. It is unclear whether divorce is better or worse for the children. Much depends on how bad is the marital relationship. Certainly if the marriage is characterized by physical or verbal abuse, physical or verbal violence, this can be devastating for the child. Unfortunately, when the marriage is so characterized, the likelihood is that there will be much continuing verbal abuse following the separation.

In such an immature relationship, the child will often become an emotional football, who will be bandied about by each one of the spouses in order to gain some form of advantage. But where such immature behavior exists during the marriage, it is not likely to change much afterwards. Arguably then, the divorce does not actually improve the welfare of the child in a significant way, but it does sometimes improve the emotional welfare of the victimized spouse.

Additionally, when the marriage is of a reasonably manageable but not thriving nature, at least overtly, the jury is still out as to whether staying in such a marriage actually disadvantages the child. There are some who argue quite vociferously that intact marriages, even though not of the most glorious type, are preferable to the most noble of divorces.

On balance, it is clear that divorce is not a panacea. It therefore behooves both individuals within the relationship to do their utmost to see if the marriage can be placed back on the proper course.

~

SHIFTING FOCUS

It is entirely possible that after having done everything one can to save the marriage, it still does not work. This is usually the case if just one of the couple is willing to cooperate in the effort. Usually, if both are willing to give their best to the effort, the chances of that effort succeeding are much greater. But when the effort is half-hearted, or when it is whole-hearted with only one of the couple, but less than half-hearted with the other, the chances of any intervention saving the marriage are quite remote.

When this happens, when the divorce becomes unavoidable because of the non-cooperation or the non-caring of one or both of the spouses, one has reached the point of no return, and the concerns switch from saving the marriage, toward saving the future.

Chapter 4

WHEN ALL ELSE FAILS

~

BASIC PRINCIPLES

One of the primary principles in the Jewish divorce ethic is that divorce is a last resort. This means that divorce should become an option only after all possibilities for maintaining the marriage have been exhausted, and the efforts to save the marriage have become irreversibly futile. To divorce with no adequate reason is considered a breach of Jewish law (See Arukh HaShulhan, Even HaEzer, 119:5). This pertains mainly when the husband divorces his wife against her will, as was possible in pre-Rabbenu Gershom times. But the intent of this prohibition remains.

There is a second principle emanating from the first; if divorce becomes a necessity, based on the realities as projected in the first principle, then there is a prescribed Jewish way to do it. The way of Jewish divorce must be predicated on appreciation of the values that should be in operation throughout the divorce process and beyond, including decency and responsibleness.

⁓

DIVORCE MODEL

A useful model for divorcing properly is provided in the Talmud (Baba Mezia, 32b). Generally, one is obliged to help others in need. Thus, one who sees another struggling to place a load on an animal must rush to help. That obligation also applies to helping the other to unload. What if two situations present themselves simultaneously, one of loading and one of unloading? The rule is that one first helps with the unloading. The reasoning is self-evident. The animal with the load is already burdened, and must be helped. The animal to be loaded has no burden yet, and can wait.

However, all this changes in one significant instance. That is when the animal to be loaded belongs to an enemy, and the animal to be unloaded belongs to a friend. Here the rule is that one must first run to help one's enemy, even if it is for loading purposes. The reason: one must break down the hate syndrome and shatter the passion for hate. By helping the enemy, you turn that person into a friend.

This rule is a useful model for divorce. Each of the divorcing couple should break the hate pattern that normally surfaces during divorce. They should shatter the normal rules of divorcing protocol, and go out of the way to help each other, so that a potential enemy may even become a friend, or at least one with whom communication is civil.

~

AFFLICTING FORBIDDEN

Jewish law forbids any individual from afflicting any other individual (Leviticus, 25:17).

Normally, the afflicting individual is one who perceives the self to be in a position of power, and thus takes advantage of a vulnerable individual. This type of affliction could pertain in a rich person/poor person dialectic, or in transactions involving widows or orphans (Exodus, 22:20–21). Others may see these unfortunate individuals as being powerless, and therefore will take advantage of them. Jewish law forbids this taking advantage, this afflicting other individuals.

One instance among many in which this type of afflicting is likely to occur is during the divorce process and beyond. The afflicting can be done in various ways. One of the more classical and well known is the use of lawyers to make life miserable for one's spouse. Although it is not always the case, usually the male is more likely to be the offending party. Afflicting may come by way of denial of access to the home, through changing the locks. It could be through failure to provide interim payments for support on time, or sometimes through failure to provide this altogether.

One of the more usual avenues of affliction is through denial of access to the children. In this type of situation, it is the wife who, if as per usual is granted custody, is the one more likely to use access as a means of afflicting the husband.

In general, when there is ill will, each one of the separating spouses uses available weapons to make life miserable for the partner. This is an act of spite, an act of revenge, sometimes an act of putting the other in his or her proper place for having started the down-cycle of negative behavior, or whatever other precipitating reason.

~

NO WINNERS

There is a crucial observation that must be made with regard to this type of debilitating dialogue between divorcing husband and wife. It is that there are no winners. Any spouse who thinks that by fixing the other's wagon they are going to win the war is living in delusion. In a war of spite, in which each tries to outdo the other, each one becomes a loser.

The loss is in the fact that the behavior pattern is one of harming others, and hurting others. Human life must be lived in terms of positive contributions to the welfare of humankind. When one veers off onto a negative tangent, it affects the entirety of life.

Additionally, it is wise to contemplate the misery that is inflicted, via the boomerang effect, upon the individual who foists misery onto others. There may be some momentary satisfaction gained from having given the other one his or her comeuppance. But it will not take long before the other comes back for the next round leading with the right; ready, willing, and eager to inflict commensurate punishment.

Needless to say, in such a scenario, not only are the participants afflicted in that their behavior becomes sub-human, but the environment in which they live is likewise affected in an adverse way. The children who grow up in an atmosphere of bitter recrimination between the parents, even if they are not directly involved in the tug of war, will nevertheless be affected by the trauma of living in such an unhappy environment.

The memory of the unhappy childhood can play a prominent role in the children's decision concerning marriage. They may decide not to marry, and even if they do decide to marry, they may enter into marriage with trepidation, fear of failure, and lack of confidence. There are millions of children who have lived through divorce, and who carry that baggage into their future, for better or for worse.

~

DOWNWARD SPIRAL

The children, when they see directly the hurt inflicted by one of the parents upon the other, will react in one of two ways. They will either overtly take sides, and then get caught in the crossfire; or else they will keep their peace, but at the price of swallowing the bitter pill of resentment for who they perceive to be the offending spouse, or spouses. Either possibility bodes ill for the future.

And it does not end with the children. The other family members are invariably dragged into the conflict, with each one of the spiteful divorcing spouses enlisting the support, even demanding the support of their respective family sides.

Thus, the in-laws, who may have become friends, or who at least co-existed relatively well, may be dragged into the war, and forced to take sides. The divorcing spouses, in order to justify the correctness of their behavior, may force their parents, who would like to remain on good terms with the grandchildren, into condemning the other side and justifying their own questionable behavior.

For no excusable reason, a simple divorce can become an all-out war between the husband and wife, the grandparents, aunts and uncles, cousins, nieces and nephews, of the conflicting sides. This is the potential and tragic end result of the downward spiral of irresponsible behavior.

THE KINDNESS ALTERNATIVE

At the other end of the behavioral spectrum, kindness always brings better results than nastiness. One is much more likely to evoke good feelings from others by being nice to them, even if one may not feel like being nice. There is no hypocrisy in behaving nicely towards someone for whom you harbor bad feelings. In actuality, this is more than not merely non-hypocrisy; it is saintliness.

The strong individual is the one who overcomes innate desires (Talmud, Avot, 4:1). These innate desires travel the broad range of human instinctual behavior, and include the natural instinct to harm those you feel have done you a bad turn. But life is too short, and the stakes are too high, to allow oneself to fall into this trap. If, following divorce, it is harmony, co-existence, peace, and manageability that are the operative concerns, and should be the operative concerns, then the behavioral strategy will be much different, and the results will be much better.

~

SHALLOW GROUNDS

Ostensibly, much of what is being stated here seems naive. After all, couples usually divorce because they cannot get along with one another. A happy divorce seems to be a contradiction in terms, although "unfortunately," in contemporary times, it is not as rare an occurrence as one might assume. There are many divorces that transpire simply because both or one of the marital unit feel that they are not growing any more in the marriage, and they want to *find themselves*, or improve themselves. They do not hate their mate. They may even have warm feelings towards their mate, but they feel it is time to move on. However, this is shallow grounds for terminating a marriage, and for thereby causing upset and hurt to others. Others include the spouse who is the victim of this assertive surge of the self-realization need, the children who are deprived of a well-integrated home life, and the remainder of the family, who must walk on eggshells between the now-separated sides.

~

CAN THEY BE FRIENDS

In reality, the reasons for divorce should be severely restricted and limited. Divorce should become operative only in situations of obvious impossibility to live together. In most instances when living together is impossible, the likelihood is that the couple does not get along. If the couple does not get along, can one logically expect that they will do in divorce and beyond what they were not able to do in marriage, namely to get along?

Surprisingly, the answer is yes. It is possible for a couple who does not get along with each other when living together to be able to get along without each other, when the relationship is not one of closeness, but one of detached communication. The couple does not get along with each other, probably because there is bad chemistry between them. This results from the fact that as a couple they are expected to be harmonious, but this harmony has not materialized, or has turned sour.

The parameters of the relationship after the termination of marriage are different. At this point in time, the couple is no longer a unit. There is no pressure to be sensitive to one another, to pour out the heart to one another, to be alert to the needs and concerns of the other. The primary concern is that the relationship should be civil, decent, and without the desire to inflict harm.

~

REALIZING THE CHANGE

It is vitally important for the couple to realize that once the reality of their having to be divorced settles in as being inevitable, the ground rules of the relationship change dramatically. This in itself is not easily achievable, but the awareness of this crucial difference changes the pressures and the expectations. It should therefore also change the fact that they did not heretofore get along well with each other.

It is not unusual for a couple who is divorcing because they did not get along well to suddenly find that they are getting along better. Surprising as it may seem, the reason for this is precisely because the nature of the relationship has changed. The demands are different, and therefore the reality changes commensurately.

The couple may then individually or collectively ask why they are now getting along well with each other; why could they not do so when they were married? But when they were married the situation was different, the ground rules were more demanding, the shared relationship was drastically deficient, and they could not manage. Now that they need not be husband and wife, and merely need to be friends, or even acquaintances who are able to speak to each other respectfully, matters can take a different, and hopefully positive, turn.

~

MAKING A GOOD BREAK

It is obvious that under normal circumstances, divorce should be much less contentious when there are no children involved. It is then much more likely that the couple could make a clean break. With children not at issue, what remains to be resolved are usually just property matters. These, once settled, are usually finished and removed from the arena of contention. The husband and wife may split the home or divide it up in another manner; they may agree to a once-and-for-all financial payment, and that will be it. If this is the agreement, then it will not take too much time for the fact of divorce to become a matter of history, and for each one of the couple to go on the way toward seeking other avenues of fulfillment.

Although this is not always the way it happens, the chances of it happening this way are greater when there are no children involved. When children are involved, the divorce is much more complicated. Custody becomes the key issue, child support becomes a matter of great concern, and visitation can be an explosive point of dispute. As well, concerns about the way the child will be raised can cause further bitter divisions. Precisely because the possibility of the divorce becoming exceedingly complicated when children are involved is more than likely, it becomes incumbent upon the divorcing husband and wife to resolve within themselves that they will be on their best behavior; if not merely because that is the right way to be, at the very least in order not to inflict irreparable harm on the children. Each undoubtedly says that the children are their primary concern, although quite often their behavior does not seem to correlate with such affirmation.

~

TAKING THE LEAD

It would be worthwhile, if not imperative, that both husband and wife take the lead in assuming the responsibility for decency in the entire process. Both husband and wife are well advised to sit down together before the divorce proceedings are under way, to agree that whatever their disagreements may be, all discussions will be conducted with civility, mutual respect, and uncompromising concern for the welfare of the children.

Lip service is always given to these fundamental concerns in a divorce situation. If the divorce procedure does not move along as smoothly as it should, invariably each one of the spouses will blame the other for having been the cause of this downturn, or unfortunate unfolding scenario. But placing of blame never rights any wrongs, or changes the atmosphere. On the contrary, once one starts to point fingers, fingers get pointed back, and instead of a focus on the issues, the divorce becomes an ego game.

The only winners of this type of nonsense are the lawyers. And surely, neither of the marital partners would feel too happy with the knowledge that their recriminations have burned holes in their pockets, with that money falling directly into the laps of willing counselors to their opposing sides.

All this is resource money that could be better spent on the welfare of the children, rather than on senseless feuding which only puts matters into regression.

~

PARTNERS WITH GOD

There are three partners involved in the bringing of any individual into this world. These partners are God, father and mother (Talmud, Kiddushin, 30b). In other words, each of these partners has a share in the entity that has come about through their union. This partnership does not terminate with divorce. Father and mother still retain their partnership, and their responsibility.

However, if they behave in an irresponsible manner, if their separation is characterized by fighting and ill will, then they create an atmosphere in which peace is not to be found. Where there is no peace, there is no God. The presence of peace is a Godly quality which must be even more present when the husband and wife, as partners, will not be able to give their collective strengths to the child or children, and will have to suffice with giving their separate strengths to the children. They dare not, through their feuding, deprive the children of the third partner, namely God.

ENCOURAGING DISRESPECT

Another important issue of Jewish ethical import in the divorce process deals with the obligation of the child to honor and respect parents. This obligation is not one-sided. It is true that the primary obligation is that the child behave respectfully toward the parents. However, the parents are forewarned against behaving in a way which will precipitate the child's disrespect for them (Shulhan Arukh, Yoreh De'ah, 249:19–20).

Thus, a parent is prohibited from hitting a child once the child reaches the age when conversational instruction is as effective a means of delivering a message as is a slap. Once a child reaches the age when it can be reasoned with, the parent who even just slaps such a child is sure to incur the child's wrath, and bring the child to a position where it will not respect, and may even pour forth venom at the parent.

The parent who behaves in such a manner transgresses the famous all-encompassing prohibition against placing a stumbling block in front of the blind (Leviticus, 19:14). Here the parent is placing a stumbling block in front of the unsuspecting child, through inciting the child to react disrespectfully towards the parent. Respect engenders respect; contempt and disrespect engender commensurate disrespect. Although the obligation to respect is primarily the child's, the parent has a significant role in this fulfillment, through the obligation to behave in a way which will elicit the child's respect.

This parental obligation pertains when the parents are living together as husband and wife, in a happy and harmonious home. It is equally true, and perhaps even more necessary to emphasize, when the parents are separating from one another, and the child or children are caught in the dramatic changeover, from family harmony to family division.

Precisely because parents who are splitting are likely to behave in a less than pleasant way, they must be aware that this unpleasantness can bring out the worst in the child. One repercussion may be that the child will lose respect for one or both of the parents, and therefore behave contemptuously and disrespectfully towards one or the other, or both. The worst is that the child may become a delinquent who sours on life in its entirety.

———

ENCOURAGING RESPECT

Parents who handle a divorce responsibly are less likely to lose the affection of their children, or their respect. Therefore, parents who behave irresponsibly in the divorce process are likewise derelict not only in their human responsibilities towards each other, but also in their responsibility to assure, to whatever extent possible, that their children behave in a respectful manner towards the parents.

All these are issues of overriding concern when husband and wife have resolved to divorce. This resolution to divorce must be accompanied with a parallel resolve to divorce as *mentschen*, as human beings who behave with the utmost of respect for each other.

However difficult this may be, the rewards of such controlled, respectful behavior are significant enough for each of the couple to swallow pride. Likewise, the consequences of the failure to behave in a responsible manner are so great as to dictate that the couple must swallow that pride, and even to do that which they do not feel like doing, or may find distasteful; because nothing is more distasteful than bitterness in the family.

Chapter 5

THE RIGHT TO DIVORCE

~

POTENTIAL FOR DIVORCE HEALTHY

The fact that a Jewish marriage can terminate via divorce is as old as the Jewish institution of marriage. This assures that marriage is not an institution comparable to being in prison with no exit. Marriage cannot be so closed-in that no matter what transpires, either husband or wife is captive to the other forever. The biblical allowance for terminating marriage via divorce serves to assure that both husband and wife will live up to their responsibilities in marriage if they want to remain in the union. The fact that failure to live up to responsibility can lead to divorce gives marriage a legally entrenched dynamism, with neither of the marital partners daring to take the marriage for granted just because it has been legally finalized. Whatever has been legally finalized can be legally undone.

Thus, the reality that divorce can terminate the marriage is healthy for the marriage itself. This does not mean that it is healthy to actually carry through with divorce; only that its potential for being exercised should convey a forceful message to the marital partners.

～

BOTH HAVE RIGHT TO SUE

If a husband or wife fails to live up to the essential components of the marriage, then the aggrieved party has the right to sue for divorce. It is a common misnomer that only the husband can do this. In fact, the biblical grounds for divorce, which include failure to provide food, clothing and marital intimacy, are spelled out in a situation wherein the deprived party is a bondwoman (and potential wife) who, having been so deprived, can enlist the services of the *Bet Din* (Rabbinical Court) to terminate the marriage (Exodus, 21:7–11). If the bondwoman, who was in a weakened position, could sue for divorce, it stands to reason that a conventional wife could do no less.

The precise dynamics of the divorce-granting procedure are a different matter, but the right to demand divorce is a privilege that is held by both husband and wife.

Each has the right to demand a divorce when the other has not lived up to basic requirements or responsibilities within marriage. But the fact that one has the right to demand a divorce does not mean that one must carry through with this right. One can simultaneously have the right to demand a divorce, but prudently refrain from exercising that right, and instead embark on a course for reconciliation.

———

AGAINST HER WILL

In biblical law, the husband had the right to divorce his wife against her will. The wife did not have an equivalent right, and this is admittedly a disparity between the husband and the wife.

However, to conclude that this shows insensitivity to the plight of the woman would be jumping to the wrong conclusion.

The biblical right of the husband to divorce his wife against her will was connected to another fact of biblical life, namely that a man was allowed to have more than one wife at a time. The woman had the right, before marriage, to insist, as one of the preconditions of marriage, that the husband take no other wife in addition to her. If the husband agreed to this, then he could not contravene this agreement without suffering the consequences.

~

ECONOMIC MARRIAGE

However, in the absence of any such agreement, or with the wife's acquiescence, a husband had the right to marry more than one wife. This created an institution which can perhaps best be called "economic marriage." It gave the women of that generation another option, namely the option to marry a husband who could support many wives, if material comfort was more important than any other consideration for the woman.

Admittedly, some women may have preferred only one husband of meager means and a life of struggle. But others may have opted for sharing a husband, if that meant that there would be fewer financial worries. Essentially, it was the woman's choice as to what type of marriage she wanted and what type of husband she preferred.

Considering also the likelihood that there would usually be fewer males than females within society, since many males died in war, this allowance of the husband to have more than one wife at the same time addressed the crucial issue of there not being enough males to take care of the female population. By allowing the option for a husband to have more than one wife, the possibility of every woman finding a suitable husband was at least not foreclosed.

KNOWING WHO IS WHO

For purely biological reasons, this type of arrangement was only possible with a "one husband-many wives" scenario. One wife with many husbands was not possible. One may conjecture that the basic reason for this is to assure that the child's parents are always identifiable. In the case of one husband and many wives, since it is the woman who is pregnant, the question of who is the mother is never an issue. And since it is the same husband, who is the father is likewise never an issue.

However, one woman and many husbands is a different situation. There the mother is well known, but who the father is will always remain a matter of conjecture. Thus the child may be placed in the uncomfortable and unacceptable position of growing up without a father, without paternal guidance and paternal financial support. Whatever the case, one should see in this not prejudice against women, but concern for the need to create stable communities comprised of clearly entrenched families.

~

NO EXIT, NO ENTRY

This allowance for the husband to have many wives would be an option most likely to be exercised by a husband who had the economic means to support the many wives he was marrying. However, the husband who supported many wives was also in a vulnerable position. Economic fluctuations could cause a collapse of his financial empire, such that maintenance of all his wives would become impossible. If the husband who had undertaken this form of marital support would be locked into this position forever, with no exit out via his own choice, he would never enter into such a union in the first place. This would foreclose a viable option for many women, taking away a possibility that would have been in the best interests of those who felt more concerned about financial considerations.

Thus, in order to make this a workable option, the men had to be given an exit out in case their financial capacities dictated this exit. The exit out was in the form of the allowance of the husband to divorce his wife against her will.

It is thus logical, although at first glance quite surprising, that within the biblical legal structure, the allowance for divorce against the will of the wife was actually consistent with the best interests of women, even though at times it could create some disadvantages to women. The intent was to maintain the viable option of economic marriage so that women would have a much broader range of choice for whom they desired to marry. Only with arbitrary exit was initial entry conceivable.

~

ENTER RABBENU GERSHOM

All this changed with the famous edicts of Rabbenu Gershom early in the twelfth century, the edicts which proscribed having more than one wife at a time, and removed the right of the husband to divorce his wife without her consent. Rabbenu Gershom, through these edicts, served to highlight, in a contemporaneous manner, the concern of the Torah for the welfare of the woman.

A combination of societal conditions and a general aversion to the practice led to the ban on having more than one wife at a time. By so doing, marriage became a purely one-to-one relationship. Economic marriage, in which a wife would share the husband with one or more women, was no more to be, except within elements of the Sephardi community who did not come under the purview of the edict, and never accepted it as binding on them. However, it is the general practice within most of the Sephardi community, the communities of the East, that the husband binds himself via oath, prior to marriage, not to marry a second time whilst married to his first wife.

~

MOVING TOWARD EQUALITY

Since being married to many women was no more to be, there was concomitantly no more reason to justify the husband's right to divorce his wife against her will. Thus, once marriage was established on a "one wife at a time" basis, the wife's rights within the marriage, and her right to terminate the marriage, were effectively raised to the level of being equal to that of the husband. He must agree to grant, and she must agree to accept, the *get*.

This was the intent of the decree of Rabbenu Gershom, to equalize the partners in marriage. His edicts may have created a different legal reality than that which existed in biblical times, but the edicts were consistent with, and an extension of the fundamental principles that were operative in biblical times. They evince a profound understanding of the letter, spirit, and intent of the biblical legislation.

Rabbenu Gershom's edicts established quite clearly that the biblical right of the husband to divorce his wife against her will is not to be seen as a biblically conferred extra power given to the husband over his wife. It is difficult to fathom that God would entrench inequity in the Torah (the revealed instruction on life), which is replete with exhortations to be attentive to all humanity, and mindful of their welfare. The aforementioned rule is rather a biblically entrenched reality designed to create greater opportunities for the women in society. Once this was no longer the case, the husband's powers in this regard were essentially removed.

~

LIMITS TO EQUALITY

Generally, although still with some exception, in divorce matters the post-Rabbenu Gershom husband and wife, at least on a legal-theoretical level, are for all intents and purposes equals. This does not mean that there are no husbands who take unfair advantage of their wives, through their refusal to grant a *get*.

Rabbenu Gershom removed the basic right of the husband to divorce his wife in a coercive way, but in *very* limited situations this ban is not enforced, or is circumvented. Thus, when the husband has a legitimate right to divorce, such as because of being childless, and the wife refuses to cooperate, or when the wife suddenly becomes apostatized, Rabbenu Gershom's edict may be circumvented through the permission (heter) of 100 Rabbis in three adjoining communities, who agree to allow the husband to remarry. But the husband must first authorize the writing of the *get*, and place that *get* in escrow at the *Bet Din*, to be delivered to the recalcitrant wife once she agrees. Thus, the husband's advantage does not become the wife's disadvantage. More importantly, the cooperation of the husband in authorizing the writing of the divorce and then transmitting it remains critical. If he refuses, the wife is severely disadvantaged, even becoming an *agunah*—an anchored, tied down, imprisoned woman, a victim of *get* abuse.

The husband's refusal to cooperate is inexcusable, abhorrent, and an abomination. It is a distortion of every basic value of human decency, and as well entails a prohibition against afflicting those individuals who are in vulnerable positions. In simple terms, refusal to grant a woman a *get* is an ethical breach of the highest order, a breach which cannot and should not be countenanced by the Jewish community.

―

COMMUNITY INTERVENTION

This means that community leadership should not allow any individual to take advantage of anyone else under any circumstances. The circumstance in which this is most likely to occur is in the area of divorce. One of the major problems in the inequities surrounding divorce is the reluctance of leadership, both Rabbinic and lay, to take a pro-active role in condemning such behavior not only in theory, but also in specific, real life situations.

Condemnation is itself more than just a lip service statement that "it is not proper," "it is incorrect," or "it is not fitting." Condemnation should take the form of denial of any honors within the community to those who have been flagrant violators of the fundamental principles of human decency, through causing affliction to the spouse. One Rabbinic organization has very recently taken significant steps in this direction.

It should also involve the readiness to publicly denounce the intransigent louts who abuse others through non-cooperation.

Denunciation can come from the pulpit, in the newspapers, or via picketing the violator's home or office. For those who do nothing or less, we should stop at nothing to heap communal contempt.

~

MESSAGE OF THE EDICTS

A husband and wife within the marriage are equals, but because of circumstances as previously described, were not equals in divorce. The edict of Rabbenu Gershom, specifically directed as it is towards re-entrenching that equality not only in theory but also in actual practice, is at the same time a message to the members of the Jewish community contemplating divorce. Divorce is not a power struggle. It is not a power game, with one spouse trying to out-muscle or out-maneuver the other. The husband and wife marry as equals, and should divorce as equals; appreciating the equality of the other, and proceeding through the divorce with equanimity.

Chapter 6

THE HUSBAND'S GROUNDS FOR DIVORCE

~

NO FAULT

The most elementary grounds for divorce is basically of the *no fault* variety. It is commonly assumed that *no fault* divorce is a late 20th century discovery, but this is not the case. Long before, Jewish law allowed for *no fault* divorce. If there were irreconcilable differences, if the couple was simply incompatible, and they decided, after all their efforts, that they could not make a life together, then divorce could be finalized.

It was not necessary to prove adultery, or any other serious charge of marital malpractice, in order for husband and wife to terminate their union. Thus, even though divorce is not a happy event, in situations of mutual agreement it can be relatively straightforward.

———

FAULT

Divorce becomes more complicated when only one of the partners wants the divorce, or demands the divorce from the other. This type of litigational complexity arises from charges by one or the other of the partners that the spouse has been derelict in marital responsibilities.

There is a precise halakhic (Judeo-legal) inventory of the circumstances when either the husband or the wife has the right to a divorce, a right which thereby obligates the other partner to cooperate. The majority of problems arise when the husband refuses to cooperate, and to a lesser degree when the wife, who now cannot be divorced against her will, refuses to cooperate. Rabbinical courts do have some muscle, but lack the real force of the *Bet Din* (Rabbinical Court) of yesteryear. Rabbinical Courts can impose sanctions, and in situations of husband or wife intransigence, it would be most helpful for the court to use all of its muscle to make sure that the couple cooperates.

～

DENIAL OF BASICS

The husband may demand the divorce if his wife denies him the benefits of conjugal visitation, what is termed in the Torah as *onah*. This is a fundamental ingredient of the marital union which, if deliberately distorted, destroys the marriage at its very root. Additionally, the wife's desertion without any just cause is also grounds for the husband demanding a divorce. In such instances, when it is clear that the wife is at fault, she also forfeits the *ketubah* (marital contract) settlement.

The *ketubah* settlement is the amount promised by the husband to the wife at marriage, should the marriage break up either through divorce, or the death of the husband.

However, when it is the wife who precipitates the break, she is not allowed to gain materially from her causing the marriage's disintegration.

These instances of non-cooperation by the wife, either through denial of *onah* or desertion, give the husband the right to divorce his wife. However, it does not confer upon the husband the responsibility to divorce his wife. It is a right which he may choose not to exercise.

~

ADULTERY

The situation of adultery is different. When there are actual eyewitnesses who testify to the wife's adultery, the husband has no choice but to divorce his wife. He may no longer live with his wife, in the face of her own brazen contempt for the sanctity of the marriage, and her failure to protect the integrity of the marriage institution. And it can be nothing but brazen contempt if the adultery took place in the presence of two eyewitnesses.

It should be understood that although adultery is a grievous breach, the type of adultery that would necessitate divorce is a rare type, that which is carried out, after forewarning, in the presence of witnesses. That type of arrogant, contemptuous adultery hardly occurs.

When it does occur, such irresponsible behavior eats away at the very fabric of Jewish life and cannot be tolerated within the marriage. Since it is the community at large that suffers from this type of behavior, neither the husband nor the wife can place themselves above the community by ignoring or sanctioning such behavior. The community is bigger than any individual or any couple.

NOT ONE-SIDED

With regard to the denial of conjugal visitation by the wife, or her leaving, whilst the grounds seem to be clear and precise, this is not always the case. It is obvious that there may be legitimate grounds for the wife denying herself to the husband.

One such justification is that the husband abuses her physically or verbally, and she therefore has only contempt for him. The husband cannot then complain that his wife refuses to engage in sexual relations.

Likewise, if the wife leaves the household because she cannot tolerate the husband's continuing physical or verbal abuse, she cannot be blamed. The husband certainly does not have a right to argue for divorce as a consequence of behavior on the wife's part that was precipitated by him.

In this, as in most other instances of contentious issues relative to the suing for divorce, the matter must be adjudicated by a competent Rabbinical Court which is able, through careful and attentive listening, to apply Jewish law to the specific circumstances.

~

ADULTERY DIFFERENT

However, adultery is another matter, for which there is no possible justification. One can understand why the husband's callousness and cruelty could make the wife feel utter revulsion for her partner in marriage, and why she thus refuses to engage in any intimate expression. However, this does not explain or excuse the wife then sharing herself with another individual outside the marriage.

True, one can understand the wife's being turned off from her husband. But in such instances, the proper thing to do is to confront the issue, and either correct it, or leave the scene permanently via divorce. The sanctity of marriage remains intact even when the marriage itself is shaky. If it were left for each individual to arbitrarily decide at which point in time the marriage is shaky enough that extra-marital relations can be pursued, then understandably the sanctity of the marital union would be destroyed.

When there is suspicion of adultery, with no direct proof or actual eyewitnesses to the adultery, but with legitimate suspicion that the adultery actually took place, the situation is more complicated. Here, the husband has the right to divorce his wife, but he is not constrained to exercise that right.

~

IMPROPER CONDUCT

There are other behaviors of the wife which would give the husband the right to divorce. They include a broad range of actions by the wife, including immodest conduct, the wife's cursing or insulting her husband, her insulting their children or the husband's parents in the presence of the husband, or the wife's hitting him.

Again here the matter is not as simple as it appears. The husband must show bad intentions on the part of the wife. He must be able to prove that her behavior was more than an isolated incident, or reaction to provocation, or even just a temper tantrum. He must be able to show that this was a calculated, well-thought-out, and pre-planned spiteful verbal or physical assault.

It is understood that if the wife's conduct in this manner is in reaction to the husband's being the instigator via his own verbal or physical abuse, or improper conduct, that he cannot then demand a divorce from his wife for behavior that he elicited.

Similarly, the husband may pursue divorce if his wife perverts him with regard to matters of Jewish law. This may pertain if she feeds him food which is not *kosher* (fit to be eaten according to Jewish law), or fools him into marital relations when she is still in a menstrual state.

Here too, the situation is not one-sided. The husband must be able to show that it was intentional religious subversion that was perpetrated by his wife. He must likewise be able to show that he really cares about these matters, that they are not merely an excuse whereby to gain divorce. Thus, a husband who digests a steady diet of cheeseburgers cannot legitimately claim that he wants a divorce because his wife gave him food that was not *kosher*.

―

IMPEDIMENTS

Another precipitant for which the husband may press for divorce is if the wife has a physical blemish which the husband finds so distasteful as to make it impossible to continue in the union.

However, here the husband may demand a divorce only if he was unaware and could not be aware of this blemish prior to the marriage. A blemish which develops only after the wedding cannot be used as grounds by the husband to press for divorce.

If the husband and wife have lived together for ten years, and they have no children, he has the right to ask for divorce, so that he should be able to remarry and attempt to fulfill his obligation for procreation. In this instance, the husband is not obliged to pursue divorce. He has this right, and also the right to refuse to exercise it (see further, Chapter 8).

These are some of the major issues of contention that may arise in marriage, and for which the husband has the right to seek a divorce.

～

SPOILING THE MEAL

Mention should be made of another possible just cause for the husband seeking a divorce. This is the situation of the wife spoiling her husband's food. Obviously, the rate of divorce would be astronomically high, and married life would be a continual pressure cooker, if every spoiled supper or burned breakfast toast could be used by the husband as an excuse for divorce.

The language of the Talmud in this situation seems to focus on the element of spite. The language of this clause is, precisely, that "she spoiled *his* food" (Gittin, 90a). This means that her own food was not spoiled, but that his was spoiled. This would indicate that the wife deliberately spoiled her husband's food but made sure that her own meal was okay. Such culinary spite speaks of the wife's purposeful setting out to ruin her husband's meal, and indicates that the marriage has reached intolerable levels.

Again here, as in most of the other instances of the husband's right to divorce, the wife can counter-attack with legitimate reasons for why she spoiled her husband's food, such as that he used offensive and foul language to her, or abused her, and she was so mad that she took it out on the vegetables or the meat. One can assume that the Rabbinical Court would have nothing but admiration for her restraint, rather than imposing the husband's unwarranted desire for divorce upon her.

~

DIVORCE NOT INSTANTANEOUS

Needless to say, just leaving the matter of an obviously conflicted marriage without intervening to get at the root of the problem would be unwise and irresponsible. When speaking of the husband having the right to seek a divorce, or of the wife's ability to counter the husband's desire for divorce, this does not imply that the Rabbinical Court will behave in a precipitous manner.

The very notion of a *get* procedure is to forestall the instantaneous termination of a marriage. The Rabbinical Court will deliberate, and the first point of deliberation will be to see if outstanding issues between the couple can or cannot be corrected. It is only after this avenue of approach has been explored and found to be futile that the court will entertain the matter of the legitimacy of the claims.

Chapter 7

THE WIFE'S GROUNDS FOR DIVORCE

~

WOMAN CAN INITIATE

The right of the wife to demand a divorce is as legally entrenched as is the right of the husband to demand a divorce. This legal entrenchment goes all the way back to biblical times, and is not merely an adjustment to more modern contingencies.

It would be a basic inequity in the relationship if the husband would be allowed to sue for divorce for whatever precipitating factor, whilst the wife would not be allowed to demand exit from the marriage no matter what happened. No one can deny that there are inequities in the system, but these inequities emanate more from abuse of the system rather than from its basic weaknesses.

~

EQUITY IN THE LAW

The very same Torah that forewarned against taking advantage of the orphan and the widow could hardly be expected to entrench vulnerability of the wife within the marriage. If anything, the sense of fairness, and concern for all individuals no matter what their position or station in life, is a central feature of the Torah. All individuals are Godly creations, and all individuals must be appreciated as such.

It is therefore not surprising and quite natural that the woman has access to exit from the marriage not only in cases of mutual desire, but also in situations when she is obviously disadvantaged by a callous and insensitive husband.

To force a woman to endure the agony of a cruel husband who abuses her is unfathom-

able. The self-same Torah of God which forbids the afflicting of others could surely not
allow, or tolerate, a situation wherein afflicting of others is permitted to continue through
the camouflage of an institutionalized union.

~

IRRESPONSIBILITY

The primary right of a woman to demand a
divorce is linked to situations when basic marital needs have been neglected, or abused by
the husband. The husband is then "convinced"
by the court to both grant the *get* to his wife,
and to give her the *ketubah* (marital contract)
settlement.

The husband who has been derelict with
regard to the sustenance that he is obliged to
give to his wife, or the conjugal visitation that
he must share with his wife, has thereby vio-
lated a primary responsibility of the marital
covenant, and the wife has the right to a
divorce in these situations. These elements of
the marriage are so crucial, that their being
used by the husband as a weapon with which

to deprive the wife, either emotionally or physically, is considered a breach of the sacred marital trust.

A woman may demand a divorce from her husband, if he has been found to be philandering with other women. There need not be proof of his having committed adultery, just of his having cavorted with other women. Even his causing her a bad name through his lecherous actions is likewise considered legitimate justification for the wife launching a divorce action. If the wife feels repulsed by her husband, it is wrong to force her to remain in the union. If the wife should make a vow that affects the marital union, such as a vow related to abstaining from conjugal union or some other impediment to marital viability, and the husband purposely fails to annul that vow, this is interpreted as a desire on his part to sever the relationship. The wife may then demand a divorce.

Should the husband, via a vow, forbid the wife to engage in any form of work, this is considered sufficient grounds for the wife to demand a *get*. The reasoning behind this is that imposed idleness has certain adverse personal consequences, leading to frustration and perhaps even worse. No wife can be coerced into such an adversity.

~

ABUSE

The husband who hits his wife, curses her, ridicules her, insults her, or insults his wife's parents in the presence of his wife, or forbids his wife from visiting her parents or family, or whose general mode of communication with his wife is through temperamental outbursts and disrespectful language, creates a situation which is untenable. The wife cannot be expected to live in such an environment, and she is well within her rights to demand a divorce.

In this situation, the wife must be able to show that this is not a rare occurrence, or an isolated outburst, but that it is reflective of the husband's usual demeanor. Should a husband counterclaim with the charge that his behavior is instigated by her, the burden of proof is upon him. We assume the correctness of the wife's position unless and until the husband can prove otherwise.

———

UNBEARABLE CONDITIONS

The woman whose husband insists that his mother (that is, the wife's mother-in-law) move into the house — and this thereby restricts the wife's freedom — may demand a divorce if this is an unbearable situation for her.

The wife whose husband forces her into conjugal relations during her menstrual period may also demand a divorce. This is the case even if she may not be scrupulous with regard to observing the laws of menstruation, which forbid conjugal union during that period and seven days beyond.

The underlying common denominator in the mother-in-law and menstrual situations is that the husband fails, or refuses, to accord to the wife the freedom, dignity and respect to which she is entitled beyond any question.

The wife has the right to demand a divorce

if the husband, for whatever reason, makes life unbearable for her. Aside from some of the reasons heretofore cited, this untenable situation may come as a result of the husband having developed a repulsive blemish, or having adopted a noxious habit, such as cigarette smoking. It may ensue from his having taken on a malodorous, offensive trade, from which he comes home with an intolerable stench.

The wife who was aware prior to marriage that her husband would be making his livelihood in an offensively smelling vocation, is still able to claim that her awareness prior to the marriage did not prepare her and condition her to live with it. Even though she had the best of intentions, it turned out that the stench was much worse than she had envisaged, and she now finds it unbearable.

~

CHILDLESSNESS

If the husband is unfortunately sterile, the wife has a right to a divorce, on the proviso that this demand for divorce is linked to her assertion that she desires to have children. The same is true if the husband is impotent. When the husband takes issue with the wife's claim that he is impotent, her statement of his impotence is considered to be the more powerful argument. She is believed as long as she makes this statement directly, and not via the "good" offices of a lawyer.

Although the grounds spelled out here do not exhaust the full gamut of legitimate right for the wife to demand a divorce, they do provide sufficient insight into the wide range of circumstances which are found to be unfair to the woman, and because of this unfairness, she is allowed to demand exit from the marital union. Much as divorce is not a desideratum within Jewish life, neither is the locking-in of either husband or wife in a prison of misery.

~

ISRAEL AND JERUSALEM

The land of Israel, a potentially explosive issue within marriage, has implications for divorce. The general rule is that whichever of the cou-

ple desires to move to Israel has the full right
to the cooperation of the other spouse in this
desire, and can demand a divorce from the
reluctant spouse, if that spouse refuses under
any circumstances to move to Israel. The
exception to this is when moving to Israel
would transform the couple into a charity
case, unable to make ends meet on their own.

The same general equation applies when the
issue is moving, within Israel, from any other
city to Jerusalem. The spouse who desires to
move to Jerusalem has the more powerful
hand, and can demand a divorce from the
intransigent other spouse who refuses the
move to Jerusalem.

The reasoning behind this is that Israel is
crucial to spiritual growth. Since marriage is a
spiritual union in which the couple should
grow together in a decidedly spiritual way, the
failure to move to Israel, or Jerusalem,
obstructs rather than facilitates this growth.
There is a transcendent quality to the marriage that is neutralized through this refusal.

Neither of the marital partners has the right
to stand in the way of the marriage taking such
a positive direction. The obstinate refusal to go

along with such an obvious incremental improvement in the marriage's spiritual content is considered to be a breach of the primary intent of the marital covenant. But it is advisable that the marital partners not use the Israel or Jerusalem factor as a weapon. This, and other marital growth issues, should be a shared concern.

~

A UNIQUE TITLE

Within the realm of claims to divorce, there is a unique title and attendant rules given to one specific situation. That is the situation when either the husband or the wife refuses to be involved in conjugal relations. In this matter, the affected party, be it husband or wife, has sufficient grounds to demand divorce. This has already been discussed.

The instigator of this refusal is given a precise title, a title of dubious distinction. The instigator is labelled as a "rebel." If it is the husband, he is referred to as a *mored*; if it is the wife, she is referred to as a *moredet*.

This term is generally accepted as applying specifically to conjugal visitation. It speaks eloquently and powerfully about the seriousness with which deviation from conjugal responsibility is viewed within the Judaic perspective. It is well known that pejorative labels are not the usual Judaic way of expressing displeasure with behavior. The use of such a label here must be seen as an extraordinary deviation from the norm, and a sharp comment on the extreme gravity of this offense. Using one's body as a weapon to punish one's partner prostitutes the marriage compact in a most serious and inexcusable way.

GENERAL RULES

The husband who is a *mored* must give his wife a divorce, and must also give her the marriage settlement known as the *ketubah*. The wife who is a *moredet* may be divorced by her husband, and she forfeits her right to the *ketubah* settlement. When it is the husband who is the *mored*, the rebellious one, the wife has the right to seek a divorce, but she is not compelled to exercise that right.

The reasoning for this is quite simple. Compelling the wife to seek a divorce would contravene the basic notion that the wife cannot be divorced against her will. It is obvious that any situation which forces the wife to seek a divorce from her husband would open up a convenient excuse for the husband to behave in that derelict manner, so as to be sure that he will gain the wife's cooperation for the divorce. This is unacceptable.

CONJUGAL GAMES

It is interesting to note that the husband is considered a rebellious one, a *mored*, even if he just swears off conjugal relations for a short period of time. He is a *mored* even if that period coincides with the wife's menstrual period, when conjugal visitation is in any event proscribed. The point being driven home with this stricture is that one's body, one's very being, may never be used as a device to punish, deprive, or threaten the other. When the relationship reduces itself to that level, the exit door is opened wide.

A husband who insists on engaging in conjugal union with his clothes on is likewise considered a rebel, a *mored*. Even though he may be motivated by considerations of modesty, and he thus may argue that this is not spiteful deprivation, it is deprivation nevertheless.

The wife who denies herself to her husband is considered a *moredet*, a rebellious wife, even if she claims that her locking the husband out of conjugal intimacy is because of the husband's debts incurred to her.

~

LIMITATIONS

Under any circumstances, the wife does not have an obligation to submit to frequent conjugal union beyond the norm. She can never be reduced to chattel, to be used by the husband at his lustful whim.

The wife is likewise not considered a *moredet* if she leaves the house because the husband

114

has failed to live up to his maintenance responsibilities. In fact, in such an instance, the husband is considered to be the instigator.

Additionally, if the wife leaves for other reasons, such as because of difficulties with her in-laws, then too she is not labelled a *moredet*, if she maintains her willingness to engage in conjugal union with her husband. The fact that she has left the premises does not necessarily mean that she has denied herself to her husband.

With regard to the extraordinary situation and label of *mored* and *moredet*, the husband and wife are equal, in that whatever legitimately removes from the one the label of rebel, would accomplish the same for the other.

～

CAN, BUT NOT OBLIGED

Having spelled out the situations and grounds for which both husband and wife can demand a divorce, it bears repeating and reemphasizing that simply because such reason or ground exists, this does not militate that either husband or wife should run to the divorce court, or more specifically, to the *Bet Din* that supervises the granting of a *get*. The first reflex in situations like this is to address the issue, to carefully scratch below the surface, to find out what exactly has triggered the overtly non-cooperative behavior of the spouses.

When true love, respect, and appreciation prevail, neither husband nor wife will deny the self to the other, or be derelict in the responsibilities to the other. The fact that they do so indicates there is something seriously wrong with the marriage. Because there is something seriously wrong with the marriage, the overriding impulse should be towards correcting that which is wrong. Radical surgery is only a last resort.

Chapter 8
THE TEN YEARS ISSUE

—

DIVORCE AMONG RELIGIOUS BITTER PILL

As a general rule, with allowance for exceptions, the more religious the couple who is divorcing, the more likely it is that their divorce will be bitter. This is an observation that comes from personal involvement with divorce, and from discussion with others who have been involved with this very painful component of Rabbinic life.

The reason for this is quite simple. Religious couples are more likely to have greater misgivings about divorcing. Though there is no denying that the divorce option is available, and biblically mandated for when a couple does split, nevertheless there is a great hesitancy to exercise that option. Marriage is sacred, and involves the sharing of a destiny by the couple.

The couple who marries within the religious sphere see their commitment as being lifelong. The idea of divorcing because one has outgrown the marriage, or because one seeks self-fulfillment via another, more challenging partner, or whatever other rationale for divorce, would simply be unacceptable for religious couples. For divorce to occur, there must have been and continues to be a serious impediment to the marriage, an impediment which defies any resolution. If it is a serious impediment, it is likely to be an anger-causing and bitterness evoking impediment.

Thus, the religious spouses who divorce are more likely to be combatants in a war; bitter enemies who drag each other down, and their families with them. When speaking about this being more likely, it does not necessarily follow that this is a certainty; only that it is more likely to be the case.

~

THE EXCEPTION

However, there is one specific exception to this general observation. This exception involves instances when the divorce takes place because of the inability of the couple to have children. According to Talmudic law, a husband who failed to fulfill his obligation to have children within the space of ten years after marriage was obliged to seek another mate with whom to fulfill this obligation (Yevamot, 64a). Following the edict of Rabbenu Gershom, which forbade the husband from having more than one wife at a time, this meant that for the husband to find another mate, he would first be obliged to divorce his present mate.

At the other end of the spectrum, the wife who was childless with her husband could likewise ask the court to arrange for her divorce to be finalized. Her argument that she wanted children, and this was why she wanted out of the marriage, would be accepted.

～

PROCREATION OBLIGATION

The primary obligation to procreate rests with the husband. Although it is the wife who does the carrying and goes through the excruciating labor and childbirth process, it is the husband who fulfills the commandment to be fruitful and multiply, through his wife giving birth.

At first glance, this seems incongruous, even unfair. After all, why is it that the wife does all the work and the husband gets all the credit?

The husband fulfills his obligation via the childbirth. The woman is not placed into the position of being obliged to have children, precisely because the process of childbirth is painful. The Torah at all times refuses to impose any commandment on an individual which by definition can only be fulfilled through pain.

～

PAIN, YOM KIPPUR, AND CIRCUMCISION

The most immediate challenges to this general principle seem to come from the obligations to fast on *Yom Kippur* (Day of Atonement) and to circumcise the child, both observances which have a pain component. But the obligation to fast on *Yom Kippur* also contains within it the attendant obligation to eat on the day beforehand, so that the ill-effects of the fast will not be so severe (Talmud, Berakhot, 8b).

The commandment to circumcise becomes obligatory when the child is eight days old. Since circumcision is a covenantal act, it would seem more appropriate that the child who is entering into the covenant do so with his full wits, namely at the age of *Bar Mitzvah* (responsible to fulfill the commandments), upon entry into the fourteenth year.

Instead, it is the parent who is obliged to arrange for the child's circumcision, and to do so at the earliest possible stage. The earliest possible time is after the child has cycled through the first seven days on his own, and has established some form of functional autonomy. The earlier the circumcision takes place, the less pain the child feels.

Thus, the principle of avoiding pain in the fulfillment of the commandment is so great that the commandment to circumcise is pushed back to the eighth day, rather than being done at the more appropriate but also more painful age of thirteen full years.

~

PAIN AND CHILDBIRTH

Likewise, since childbirth is painful, the primary onus for having children is placed upon the man, for whom childbirth is certainly free from pain. However, once the obligation is placed upon the husband, this carries with it certain weighty responsibilities. These include his obligation to be attentive to that requirement, and to take drastic measures if he has not fulfilled his obligation within ten years after marriage.

The couple who is childless has not necessarily drifted apart. On the contrary, they may have been brought even closer together through their common effort to beget children. This is an exceptional circumstance, wherein the couple may part company even though they love each other dearly. But they have failed in their intense desire to generate a posterity.

~

PAIN OF CHILDLESSNESS

Although Talmudic law places an onus upon the husband to find other avenues for fulfilling his obligation to procreate, the general practice now is that the husband maintains the right to ask for a divorce, but he also has the right not to exercise that right.

The wife cannot claim that she desires a divorce in order to fulfill her obligation to procreate, since she does not have such a direct obligation. However, she is well within her rights if she asks for divorce on the grounds that having children is important to her, independent of whether it is obligatory.

It is a matter of *halakhic* (Judeo-legal) give-and-take, whether the husband can force the issue concerning the divorce under these circumstances. In the face of the wife's refusal to cooperate, it is debatable whether the edict of Rabbenu Gershom proscribing divorce against the wife's will can be circumvented through the permission of one hundred Rabbis.

What is beyond debate is that this is an excruciatingly painful type of divorce. It is painful because it is a divorce that is really not desired by either of the parties, were it not for the overwhelming wish to have children that neither of them has been able to fulfill.

The husband who goes to court asking for a divorce on the grounds of being childless, but who does so after having had a feud with his wife, is looked upon with some suspicion. This is a grounds for divorce that, to be claimed, must not involve any rancor between the divorcing couple.

This explicit precondition just about guarantees that the divorcing couple will have affectionate feelings towards one another when going through the painful process of separation.

—

TEN FUNCTIONAL YEARS

The ten year waiting period is more than it appears to be at first glance. These ten years must be ten years in which the husband and wife live together normally as husband and wife. Thus, if the husband was away for whatever reason for a protracted period of time, this does not enter into the calculation as part of the ten year wait.

Additionally, if there was a period of time during which there were no normal husband-wife relations, for whatever reason, medical or otherwise, this time period also does not enter into the equation. If the husband and wife were in an obvious state of disease, or tension, such that normal husband-wife relations were not possible, this period of time is removed from the ten year requirement.

The years in which either one of the couple was sick are also not included in the ten years. The sickness itself may have been the cause for the childlessness during that period, and cannot be considered as part of the ten years.

In other words, the ten year period must be

ten years in which just about any other causes
for the marital union not resulting in any offspring have been precluded. Failing that, we
are not adequately assured that having children is beyond hope.

~

MODERN MEDICINE

Whilst ten years is the period of time that is
given in the Talmud, with modern technology
it is possible to ascertain even earlier whether
in fact the couple will be able to have children. It is also possible to more precisely pinpoint who of the couple is the one more
responsible for the failure to have children.
Surely, if the medical evidence shows that it is
the husband's infertility which causes the couple to be childless, he can then hardly ask the
court to intercede on his behalf for a divorce.
If he is the cause of the childlessness, there is
no hope that he will have children from
another marriage. He then has very shaky
grounds upon which to ask for a divorce.

On the other hand, when it is clear that it is

the husband whose condition causes the couple's infertility, the wife would have ample justification for seeking a *get*.

This justification would be operative once medical evidence is in, even if it is well before ten years of marriage have elapsed. In all instances when the *get* request is made because of childlessness, whether by the husband or the wife, the Rabbinical Court will surely ascertain whether the couple has made use of the extraordinary medical facilities that are today available, to see if some medical intervention would help to solve whatever problem either or both of the couple have.

It is a singular act of bad faith, and a dereliction of responsibility, for either of the couple to ask for a divorce on the grounds of childlessness, but yet to have done nothing more than wait for a number of years. Without clear evidence of active investigation of all the medical possibilities, the request for divorce on the grounds of childlessness will be viewed as less than credible.

~

ADOPTION OPTION

One can have nothing but sympathy and compassion for a husband and wife who love each other dearly, but who are now mired in the agonizingly complex and difficult trauma of having to choose between the possibilities for future posterity, versus a present love that must be sacrificed in order to gain that posterity. Nothing in life is a sure thing. There is no guarantee that the second marriage will yield better results than the first one. Yet, the overwhelming desire for children, be it by the husband or the wife, can be such a powerful motivating factor that the existent love is placed into a secondary position. This does not mean that the couple's love for each other is now placed in doubt. That love may be beyond question, yet the yearning for children may be too strong a force for the couple to stay together with no prospect for having children.

In such situations, there are some couples who explore the adoption possibilities. But this is often fraught with difficulties, with frustrations, sometimes with exorbitant expense. There is also the nagging possibility that the original mother, who had previously asserted her unquestioned willingness and firm desire to give up the child, may change her mind right after childbirth, or perhaps even a few weeks later, after the child has already been brought into the new parental home.

One can therefore appreciate the reluctance of a childless couple to explore the adoption route. No one has the right to make value judgments, or pejorative statements about a couple who, with great difficulty, even with excruciating pain, decides to part company and explore other possibilities for having children.

~

FUTURE FOCUS

In most instances of divorce, there is a lament of what went wrong in the past. The divorce that results from the couple being childless is a lament of a marriage that has no future posterity. The childless couple who divorces should not allow the divorce to neutralize the feelings that they have for one another.

Since they do love each other, and would have loved nothing more than to spend an entire life together raising and nurturing a family, their focus should now be in two directions. For themselves, they should hope that they find a mate with whom they will be able to have children. And for their beloved ex-partner, they should hope for that very same thing, that the ex-mate finds a partner with whom to build a life and a future together.

Chapter 9

THE *GET* PROCEDURE

~

UNFAIR DISPARITY

There is an obvious anomaly concerning the *get* procedure, an anomaly that is manifest in all countries outside Israel.

This is the reality that a Rabbi who is authorized by the appropriate authority can supervise and finalize a marriage, with that marriage being recognized by the state and country in which it is performed as legally binding.

However, that very Rabbi, or other Rabbinic authority, is as a general rule never given the right to terminate such marriage through the *get* procedure.

In other words, a couple who is married by a Rabbi, and through the marriage arranged by the Rabbi had both the religious and secular requirements fulfilled, cannot terminate the marriage in that self-same manner. When it comes to divorce, the religious and the secular do not meet. The secular requirements for divorce must be finalized in a civil court.

It should be noted that until a few generations ago, a religious divorce was recognized as valid by the courts. Marriage and divorce (which was quite rare) were in the hands of the religious authorities until relatively recently, when civil divorce became a possibility. Governments began to legislate divorce laws, and now civil divorce is a generally prevailing requisite even for those who receive a religious divorce.

~

DIVORCE AS HAVDALAH

This means that when it comes to divorce, the couple must go through two procedures. In addition to the secular divorce, the couple must go through the procedure of a religious divorce, a *get*. The religious divorce serves to terminate the sanctity of the union at the other end, much as *havdalah*, or the separation ceremony at the end of *Shabbat* (Sabbath) or *Yom Tov* (Festival) brings to an end the sanctity of the special day.

Anything that is sacred is sacred at both ends. A sacred day is sanctified at the outset via *Kiddush* (sanctification), and its sanctity is terminated via a separation (*havdalah*), a disjoining of the day from the ordinary. Sanctity does not evaporate on its own. Marriage too, as a sacred union, is sanctified at both ends; through *Kiddushin* and *Nisuin* (Sanctification and Uplifting) to bind the union, and a *get* to dissolve the union.

THE ISRAEL REALITY

In Israel, a divorce which is finalized in Rabbinical Court is recognized as binding, and accepted as divorce for all purposes. And, at the risk of Israel becoming a Las Vegas or Mexico, a couple who goes to Israel and resides there for the necessary length of time to establish residence by prescribed statute, and then is divorced via a Rabbinical Court in Israel, could then have that divorce accepted in other countries as the legally binding civil divorce.

The fact that the secular courts do not recognize the Rabbinical Court when it comes to divorce is unfortunate, since such recognition could alleviate the burden of the divorcing couple, and also significantly cut down the legal expenses that are incurred at the time of the dissolution of the marriage. Additionally, the prospect that a Rabbinical Court can dissolve the marriage in all its aspects would serve to increase the chances that the couple would divorce via Jewish law, rather than submit their claims and counter-claims to a civil court, whose parameters of judgment often run contrary to Jewish law.

~

CRITICAL DIFFERENCE

There is a critical difference between the divorce procedure in a civil court, and the divorce procedure that unfolds in a Rabbinical Court. In a civil court, the couple who seeks a divorce is pronounced as divorced by the court. It is the court, through its power, which decrees that the husband and wife are no longer a marital unit. However, in a *Bet Din*, the supervising Rabbis are not the ones who pronounce husband and wife as divorced. The divorce action is effected through the wife accepting the bill of divorce, called *get*, from her husband. The Rabbinical Court gives its imprimatur to the fact that the divorce has been carried out properly, and that it is therefore in effect. But they do not make a pronouncement by decree; they make a pronouncement about an act that has taken place between the two litigants, husband and wife.

This does not mean that the Rabbinical Court is a non-participant in the events that unfold. They are quite actively involved, but their active involvement is to assure and to

135

ensure that the procedure of divorce takes place properly.

~

STRAIGHTFORWARD PROCEDURE

The divorce, or *get* procedure, is relatively simple. It involves the husband instructing a scribe (*sofer*), in the presence of the presiding *Bet Din* (Rabbinical Court), to write a Bill of Divorce, a *get*, on his behalf, for his wife. The scribe undertakes this charge of the husband, and writes the *get*. The Bill of Divorce, the *get*, is then given by the husband to his wife in the presence of the Rabbinical Tribunal of three individuals, and two witnesses to the actual transmission of the divorce from the husband to the wife.

This, essentially, is the divorce procedure. However, there are many attendant details that enter into the picture, and these should be explained.

~

PRECISE REQUISITES

Firstly, the scribe must write the divorce specifically for the husband who is making the request, and for his wife. This must be the scribe's intention. If per chance there is another couple in the city who come for a divorce a few days later who by coincidence have identical names, this divorce cannot be used for them, if for whatever reason it had not yet been used. Each divorce is reserved exclusively for the couple for whom it had been written.

The Rabbinical Court, for its part, takes great pains to be one hundred percent sure about the exact names of the couple that is involved. The meticulousness with which this is approached is sometimes unnerving to the couple, but is essential to the divorce procedure.

The couple must be aware even beforehand, that any responsible Rabbinical Court takes the matter of divorce very seriously, and looks upon the *get*, as well as the procedure of transmitting the *get*, as sacred. It is sacred because it is via this *get* that the *mitzvah* (command-ment), the obligation to separate via a *get*, is fulfilled.

~

A MITZVAH

It does sound odd that to divorce one's wife is a *mitzvah*, a fulfillment of a sacred obligation. However, it is not a *mitzvah* that one must run after, such as the *mitzvah* to give charity, or the *mitzvah* to place a *mezuzah* (parchment scroll of biblical excerpts), on one's door.

This is a *mitzvah* of a conditional nature, much along the lines of the *mitzvah* to prop-erly prepare an animal before eating it. If one refrains from eating meat, then there is no rea-son to fulfill this commandment. But if one desires to eat meat, then the only way to do so is via the prescribed procedure known as *she-hitah*, or ritual preparation of the animal.

Similarly, when the couple has reached the stage wherein divorce is the only alternative, then it is a *mitzvah* to do so via a *get*. Marriage is holy, and its holiness endures to the very last moment, inclusive.

⁓

WITH FULL WITS

The scribe, the *sofer*, who is to write the *get*, gives the quill, ink, and paper to the husband. The husband, having "acquired" these basic ingredients for writing the *get*, then gives these items back to the scribe, asking the scribe to write "his" (the husband's) *get* with his (the husband's) materials.

A matter of overriding concern to the Rabbinical Court in the granting of the divorce is the need to be reassured that both husband and wife are involved in this procedure of their own free will. Questions will be asked of both the husband and wife, to assure that the husband is giving the *get* and the wife is accepting the *get* free from duress or coercion, and also free from any sworn undertaking that may have the effect of being under duress or coercion.

This is vital because the element of free willingness in divorce is critical.

The husband who delegates the scribe to write the Bill of Divorce must assure the court that he is doing so with his full wits and with his free will. Before the wife accepts the Bill of Divorce, she likewise must reassure the court that she is accepting this Bill of Divorce of her own free will, and is not being forced into it.

~

PROOF OF DIVORCE

The *get*, which is a document written in *Torah* (Five Books of Moses on parchment scroll) type script on twelve lines, twelve lines being the hebrew numerical equivalent of the word *get* (gt; g-gimmel = 3, t-tet = 9), is then given by the husband to the wife. The wife takes the *get*, lifts it up, and walks with it a little bit to indicate having taken title to it. The *get* is then read aloud by the Rabbinical Court once again, it having been read previously in the divorce procedure. It is then cut, to prevent its being used again, and put away.

Both husband and wife are then given a document which is known as a *ptur*. This document, signed by all the members of the Rabbinical tribunal, testifies to the fact that the divorce between the husband and wife has been finalized, and each is free to pursue other marital possibilities.

Often, the wife is disappointed that the very document through which she has been divorced is not retained by her, as is the case with the *ketubah*, but this is not an issue of concern. However, it does help to know in advance that the document of divorce is not the document of proof of divorce.

~

ALWAYS TRAUMATIC

The divorce procedure is relatively straightforward, and when compared with the more complicated procedure that is involved in the civil divorce, stands out for its relative simplicity. However, the fact that the divorce procedure is relatively simple does not mean that it is not traumatic.

Experience has shown that the procedure, even though entered into by the full agreement of the husband and wife, is a traumatic event. It could hardly be otherwise. The divorce carries with it many emotion-laden feelings, not the least of which is the feeling that so many years of life have been wasted; that an investment in time and emotion has gone awry.

It is quite likely that even a spouse who is eagerly looking forward to getting rid of a terrible mate will still be overcome with emotion at the time of the divorce. This is so because it brings back all the memories of the terrible marriage, and all that had been endured over a protracted period of time.

Usually, the husband handles this situation with less difficulty than the wife. This does not mean that the husband feels less affected; only that often the male feels constrained to put up a brave front to maintain the male macho image of imperviousness to emotional feelings. The wife, on the other hand, almost invariably is emotionally overcome at the divorce proceedings.

———

CONTINUING RESPONSIBILITY

The Talmud urges the husband to be extremely sensitive to the vulnerability of his wife, and to the reality that any pain that is inflicted upon her may cause her to cry (Baba Mezia, 59a). This is an ethical imperative within marriage that continues to the very end. Specifically with regard to the divorce procedure, it speaks of the husband's obligation to be sensitive to the wife's feelings at the time of the divorce.

Divorcing is painful enough as it is. The husband's insensitive, callous, or biting attitude at that point in time only makes matters worse, and is effectively a breach of his ethical responsibilities as a husband, which do not end until after the divorce is finalized. The wife too should avoid comments or gestures which pour salt on open wounds.

~

COURT SENSITIVITY

Likewise, the Rabbinical Court must be singularly aware of the sensitivity of the wife who is receiving the divorce, and must take great pains to assure that the divorce procedure does not leave the wife permanently traumatized, through her being treated more as an object than as a human being.

The Rabbinical Court has an obligation to properly carry out not only the legal details of the divorce procedure; it must also be attentive to the ethical, person-to-person responsibilities. The ways of the *Torah* are the ways of pleasantness (Proverbs, 3:17). The ways of the *Torah* must be so pleasant that even in unpleasant circumstances, they project an aura of pleasantness.

The members of the Rabbinical Court dare not, in their attention to legal detail, overlook their obligation to human detail.

~

HELPFUL GESTURES

How can a Rabbinical Court help to make the divorce procedure more pleasant? The first thing that the Rabbinical Court invariably must do is to assure that the divorcing husband and wife feel comfortable. Inquiring of their welfare, asking how they feel, offering a glass of water, are all helpful approaches which will personalize the encounter, and raise it up from being a simple legal transaction.

Another helpful gesture on the part of the Rabbinical tribunal would be to reassure the husband and wife that the procedure is harmless and painless. They should explain in advance the significance of the *get*, the nature of the procedure and its importance, and exactly what will take place during the procedure. Quite often, the anxiety of the woman in anticipation of the divorce process is related to the normal anxiety associated with venturing into the realm of the unknown. The divorce is traumatic even with all its details known in advance. But with some of the unknown elements becoming clear, the level of trauma is significantly reduced.

The Rabbis may, in advance, suggest to both husband and wife that they each bring along a friend to be at the respective sides, and reading material to help pass the time when the divorce is being written.

~

PROXY

There is another interesting nuance to the *get* procedure which can serve to reduce some of the trauma. Especially in instances when the divorce is less than amicable, it is possible for the husband and wife to take care of their specific roles within the divorce procedure without actually seeing each other.

In other words, the husband can delegate the scribe to write the divorce, and at the same time also delegate an agent, who acts on his behalf, as a surrogate husband, to deliver the *get* to his wife. In this way, the wife can be spared the further agony of having to confront the estranged spouse during the actual delivery of the divorce. It should be noted that Rabbinical Courts generally try to avoid this type of vicarious delivery.

This particular nuance within the divorce procedure is also quite useful in instances when the husband and wife who have been separated now live in different cities, such that the actual direct transmission of the divorce is complicated. Sending it via the mail from the presiding *Bet Din* for writing the divorce, to the *Bet Din* for the transmission of the divorce, serves to overcome the geographic barriers, and makes a complicated circumstance much more simple.

This type of approach to the divorce situation works on a transcontinental basis, creating a global nexus whereby a *get* can be delivered from any place to any place.

In cases when the divorce is delivered to the transmitting *Bet Din,* or other circumstances for which a surrogate husband is used, there is documentation that is read in the course of the *get* procedure, verifying the appointment of a surrogate to act on the husband's behalf.

~

POST-DIVORCE RESTRICTIONS

The divorce is final at the precise moment the wife accepts the divorce. Sometimes, especially when the divorce is delivered in a different city from where the *get* was written, it may take a few days before the wife receives the *ptur* document. However, she is effectively considered divorced from the time of acceptance of the divorce document, the *get*.

The husband and wife who have divorced are allowed to remarry each other, as long as the divorcing husband is not a *kohen* (member of the priestly family). A *kohen* is not permitted to marry a divorcee. Even though here it would be the *kohen* reuniting with the woman he himself divorced, he still is not permitted to remarry her. However, as long as the husband is not a *kohen*, and the wife has not married someone else after the divorce, the couple, if in fact they do reconcile, would be permitted to remarry.

Under normal circumstances, the woman who is divorced may not remarry for 92 days after the granting of the divorce. This includes the day of transmission of the divorce plus the day of the marriage itself, so that there is a full 90 day interval between divorce and remarriage.

Although this stricture does not apply to men, the rule is in no way indicative of a bias against women. This proviso is a precaution to prevent a case of dubious paternity.

~

REMOVING DOUBT

Simply put, should the divorced wife become pregnant within the next few months, having remarried almost immediately after the divorce, it will be impossible to discern whether her child is a nine month baby from the first husband, or a seven month baby from the second husband. Because the true paternal partner will not be known, the child will be in the untenable position of not knowing who is the real father.

That doubt will effectively deprive the child of the paternal guidance the child needs throughout life, aside of course from the child being deprived of the financial support that is the obligation of the father. Each possible father can legitimately claim that it is the other one who is the real father, and is the one who has the attendant financial obligations. The child falls into the cracks.

In order to prevent this, the simple enactment of waiting 90 days before remarrying creates the time interval that assures precise knowledge of who is the paternal parent. Should the divorced wife have a child within seven months after remarrying, it will be obvious that this child is from her second husband, since they had already passed through a three month interval.

A major exception to this proviso concerning having to wait after the divorce is when the divorcing husband and wife decide to remarry each other. Should they remarry, they can do so even within those 90 days, since the first husband and the second husband are actually one and the same. We therefore know without doubt who is the father.

∼

NO INTRUSION

Under normal circumstances, aside from husband and wife remarrying, the 90 day wait is a constant. The argument of the woman that she is not pregnant, or that she is too old to conceive, is not considered relevant to the issue. The reason for this is quite simple. We do not desire to delve into the more intimate questions of a woman's internal status, and decide questions of can she or can she not. By making this an across-the-board regulation without exception, we protect the dignity of the lady involved, and do not investigate matters which belong strictly in the realm of the personal.

Exception can be made in situations when the husband and wife have been legally divorced or separated for a while, and the wife just reminded herself that before she remarries she needs a divorce. In such circumstance, the fact of the legal separation, though only from a civil law perspective, may be separation enough to allow for a waiving of the 90 day waiting period.

~

DO NOT DELAY

As an important aside, a couple who is divorcing should not delay obtaining a *get*. They
may understandably give more attention to
the civil side, and the settling of financial and
custodial issues. However, they should take
care of the *get* immediately, even before the
civil procedure is finalized. Either of the couple who waits until just before remarrying to
obtain a *get* risks dealing with a former spouse
now possibly jealous of the other's new-found
happiness, and unwilling to contribute to it by
being cooperative.

This, in general, is the divorce procedure,
with its main components and its main implications. The exact manner in which the procedure is carried through is slightly more complicated, because there are many details that
must be satisfied, but the most important concerns in the carrying through of a divorce are
that it be done in strict conformity with Jewish
law, and according to the sensitivities that are
a basic component of Jewish ethics.

Chapter 10

HOW NOT TO DIVORCE

~

MUTUAL DISADVANTAGE

After having spelled out the basic conditions that should persist prior to divorce, and the methodology through which the divorce transaction is actually carried out, it is appropriate to delineate how not to divorce, or what should be avoided in the process of finalizing the divorce.

The divorce arena should never be used as a battleground, with both husband and wife vying for victory against the other, to gain a conquest in divorce that will more-or-less compensate for the failure of the marriage. When each seeks to be a victor, both become losers.

It is generally the case that people marry with a view that each will gain from the mutual attachment. When the couple divorces, it should similarly be with the view that neither will gain at the expense of the other in the marital detachment. In other words, whereas marriage is a situation of mutual advantage, divorce should be perceived as a case of mutual disadvantage, mutual disadvantage which is shared equally.

—

MARITAL RAPE

Advantage taking when divorce becomes inevitable is totally out of bounds. Thus, a husband who has made up his mind that the marriage is finished and he will soon be going to initiate divorce proceedings, cannot camouflage this from his wife, and then seduce her into conjugal union, or even into performing household duties. One would assume that a wife who is aware that her husband intends to divorce her will feel a sense of revulsion at engaging in marital relations. The husband who withholds his intentions from his wife, through his deceit, engages in what must appropriately be termed marital rape, or marital seduction. It is out of bounds, and considered by Jewish law as completely unacceptable behavior.

In other words, once the intention to divorce is made, neither one is allowed to take advantage of the other.

—

DOUBLE LOSS

In a divorce which is bitter, and most have some bitterness, the likelihood is that each one of the marital partners will feel victimized by the behavior of the other. Each will then have a strong desire to contest whatever is the final arrangement between the two. No one wants to lose twice. The feeling that the marriage was a lost cause, and now in the divorce one has lost again, can be quite devastating. It is natural that each one of the marital partners should desire to snatch some saving grace from what was a bad situation. It may be natural, but it is certainly not advisable.

The couple is always best advised to look upon a marriage gone sour as a collective venture that went sour. The pointing of fingers, the blaming of others, does not help; in fact, it hinders.

~

BLAMING FUTILE

As a general rule, human beings have a unique capacity to be quite perceptive when it comes to recognizing the faults of others, but are almost totally blind when it comes to seeing their own faults. All blemishes one is able to see, except one's own (variation on a statement in Talmud, Nega'im, 2:5).

One of the partners may have started the down cycle, but the other one finished. Who is to say that the one who initiated the problem is more guilty than the one who carried the problem to its ultimate, unfortunate end? How does one gauge whether the initiating of a problem, or the negative reaction thereto, comprises 25, 45, or 80 percent of the blame for the situation. Assessing relative blame is literally a no-win enterprise. At the same time, it is also an enterprise with no scientific precision attached to it. No one can know for certain, not even the parties involved. It is therefore best to avoid altogether the blaming of the other.

There are objective realities which legitimize either the husband or the wife having the right to demand the divorce. The *Bet Din*, in assessing the situation, will want to hear both sides of the story in order to get at the truth. However, they will certainly not encourage a finger-pointing debate. They will wisely deal mainly with the facts, and with who is responsible. But the recriminatory debate over who is to blame will hopefully be averted.

If the situation is untenable, and not correctable, trying to pinpoint blame is an exercise in futility. With the marital situation being hopeless, the best the couple can do is to make sure the divorce situation is not as hopeless and as frustrating as the marriage.

～

SUCCESSFUL DIVORCE

The couple should take the attitude that if their marriage failed for whatever reason or reasons, then at the very least they should try to make their divorce a success. Yes, it is possible to speak in terms of successful divorce.

What is a successful divorce? A successful divorce is a divorce in which both husband and wife detach from one another according to the basic prescriptions of Jewish law, and with a view towards terminating the marriage in as decent and humane a manner as possible. Bitter feelings may reside within the pit of each one's innards, but this does not mean that such bitterness must be translated into loud-mouthed invective. Recriminations may be harbored, but this does not mean that such feelings must be lambasted at each other.

It can be readily assumed that each one of the marital partners does have some negative feelings for the other spouse, no matter how amiable the divorce may be. Each one of the spouses should not live with the delusion that the overtly calm and friendly behavior of the

other implies that the other is perfectly at ease
with what is unfolding. On the contrary, each
should assume that the other is uncomfortable
and uneasy about what is happening. But in
the divorce there is a shared uneasiness, a
shared swallowing of pride, for the purpose of
getting on with life in as manageable a form as
is possible.

THE WRONG COURT

The accent in divorce should be not on contest-
ing the divorce, but rather on peacefully dis-
solving the marriage. Outside Israel, there are
outstanding matters that must be channelled
through a civil court. But this does not mean
that there must be contentious litigation
between the ex-partners. Dragging the divorce
procedure and its long-range implications, be
they custodial or financial, into the courts, can
involve a serious contravention of Jewish law.
Should the court decide these matters in a way
which is inconsistent with Jewish law, then the
parties involved, or the party that has dragged

this matter into the civil court, is guilty of a most serious breach. It will become clear in the ensuing chapters what are the precise financial and custodial guidelines according to Jewish law. The precise rules in this regard do not necessarily conform with the way a judge would see it. The imposing of secular categories on the post-divorce situation of the Jewish couple is, simply put, fundamentally wrong.

Each of the couple is well advised to approach a Rabbi or a religious adviser whom they trust, and who is aware of Jewish law, to advise them on how they should best approach the situation. The settlement they mutually agree to, in the best interests of all the parties involved, including the divorcing spouses and their offspring, is perfectly acceptable in civil law, and even in Jewish law. This is true provided that their agreement is not a flagrant violation of fundamental Jewish principles regarding the post-divorce reality.

~

MEDIATION

Both marital partners should mutually resolve between themselves to use this delicate balance of Rabbinic advice and legal incorporation of that legal advice as the basis for their marital separation. By so doing, each will have served to make the best of a bad situation. This will thus help to smooth the path for a future in which, though they may be separated, they are not totally disassociated, especially in situations when children are involved.

A settlement to which the couple agrees, and which is legally entrenched through the good office of lawyers who seek to resolve differences, rather than fatten their pockets by urging each of the couple to fight the other, is the best stratagem for divorce.

Thus, the couple, in choosing the path of mediation toward resolution rather than disputation and contestation, should choose lawyers with well-earned reputations for looking out for the best interests of the situation, rather than just merely the best interests of their own client. Usually, looking out for the best interests of the client translates into looking out for the best interests of the lawyer. This is a pitfall which must be avoided. The lawyers to choose are the ones with a long-range view of the future, with an understanding of the often tragic effects of bitter litigation, and the need to avoid such strife.

~

RABBINIC MALPRACTICE

The couple should reject any advice which dissuades them from the necessity of arranging a *get*. There are some religious leaders who wrongly advise the couple that they do not need a *get*, and the couple think that this is legitimate advice simply because it was told to them by a Rabbi. There are Rabbis around who do purvey this type of nonsense. Such Rabbinic malpractice must be categorically condemned, and not accepted by the divorcing couple. The fact is that in Jewish law, remarrying without a *get* creates great problems for the couple who are marrying, and for their progeny. The relationship itself is considered illicit, and the children that are born from that relationship could well be illegitimate.

The intent is not to punish the child, but to drive home to the couple that an illicit relationship begets illicit results. What is produced by an illegitimate relationship is illegitimate. It should drive home with overwhelming force to the contemplating couple that the relationship itself is illegitimate. The relationship should not be entered into until it is legitimized via the finalizing of a *get*.

~

SERIOUS REPERCUSSIONS

It should be noted that a husband who remarries without the benefit of a *get* is not in as serious a position as a woman who remarries without same. The husband who remarries without cooperating in the *get* process has obviously done wrong. Any Rabbi who supervises such a marriage deserves to be categorically condemned and treated with contempt.

However, since in original Jewish law a man was allowed to have more than one wife at a time, one cannot impose illegitimacy on the children of such a relationship. It has already been pointed out that the right of the husband to have more than one wife at a time was essentially an advantage to the woman, but sometimes advantages do translate into disparities.

On the other hand, a woman who remarries without the benefit of a *get* from the previous marriage is in a much worse situation. Aside from the fact that marrying without a divorce is adultery, by the next husband and the *get*-less wife, the child or children that are born from such a marriage are basically illegitimate, since the wife has not been legally divorced from her first husband. The woman in Jewish law can never have more than one husband at a time. The remarrying wife, who has no divorce, effectively has more than one husband at a time.

No one goes out of the way to uncover illegitimacy, or to bandy about the label of illegitimacy. Illegitimacy is a reality that is to be avoided at all costs. This means that both husband and wife who are divorcing must understand the gravity of their refusal to cooperate in the *get* process. The community as a whole should give zero tolerance to any efforts by husband or wife to obstruct the *get* process. Concomitantly, it should give zero tolerance to any religious leaders who likewise blunt the *get* process.

~

THE RIGHT RABBINICAL COURT

Husband and wife should seek out a Rabbinical Court which is authenticated insofar as Jewish divorce is concerned. It is wrong to avoid giving a *get*. It is likewise wrong to become involved with a bogus court when it comes to the delivery of a *get*. Buyer beware pertains to the choosing of the right advisers, lawyers, and Rabbis to guide the couple through the divorce process, as much as it does to any other serious consumer enterprises. A court which is not universally recognized should be avoided.

Additionally, and perhaps a bit more controversially, the couple should avoid having anything to do with a Rabbinical Court which, however well versed it may be in the nuances of Jewish law, treats the couple, and especially the woman, in a disrespectful, insensitive manner. Too many women have avoided or refused to cooperate in the granting of a *get* because of fears they harbor about this process. They have heard reports, perhaps somewhat inaccurate or exaggerated, but at times all too precise, about how callously the woman is handled by the supervising *Bet Din* when it comes to divorce.

There are enough Rabbinical courts of immaculate standing and acceptance who are sensitive to the unique situation of the woman, that one need not and should not go to a court which behaves otherwise. If courts which do not treat women respectfully are boycotted, they will then get the message. Or, if they still do not get the message, they will close down for lack of activity.

Rabbinical Courts which, however precise in their knowledge of the details of divorce, are inhumane when it comes to the personal encounter, misrepresent Judaism. They are counterproductive to the urgent need, in this age of increasing divorce, that the divorce procedure be as palatable, as full of understanding and empathy, as possible.

~

THE UPRIGHT WAY

Thus the general guideline, with regard to the divorce process, is that those involved, including the husband, the wife, the Rabbinical tribunal, and the lawyers, be of one mind in their resolve that the divorce be handled in the humane, delicate and sensitive manner that it by right ought to be.

To the contention that may be leveled at this suggestion; namely—how can one expect a divorce to go smoothly if the couple is bitter towards one another and would like to be vengeful, vindictive, and spiteful?—the theoretical answer is very simple. It is no trick to be nice when things are going well. The general overall Judaic obligation to do that which is upright and good (Deuteronomy, 6:18), to go in the way of goodness, is an ethical imperative, and a challenge that is truly fulfilled in trying times, in times when one would want to do the very opposite.

That is the theory. Is it too much to ask that this profound theory be carried out in practice?

It is useful to always keep in mind the biblical prohibition forbidding hating anyone (Leviticus, 19:17), and the further, less well-known regulation, not to be self-righteous, to think that everyone else is wrong and only you are right (see Sefer Haredim, p.91, to Deuteronomy, 9:5). By honestly incorporating these two principles, one will be well on the way towards actualizing the "upright and good" alternative in the divorce process.

Chapter 11

POST-DIVORCE FINANCIAL OBLIGATIONS

~

THE KETUBAH

One of the more complicated matters in the finalization of divorce is the establishment of the precise obligations of support following divorce.

Generally, in situations when the divorce is by mutual consent, or in the absence of any flagrant abuse by the wife, such as adultery, the finalization of the divorce also includes the wife's receiving the *ketubah* payment.

Outside Israel, this is a paltry sum, two hundred *zuz* (coins), which for all intents and purposes does not amount to very much. These two hundred *zuz* range in value from less than one-hundred dollars to, at the most, a few thousand dollars. As protection for the wife, it does not make for a strong shield.

In Israel, the *ketubah* itself contains an extra clause, containing an undertaking by the husband that should the marriage terminate either by a divorce or by the husband's death, he will grant the wife a more significant amount, based of course on the husband's ability to pay.

~

POST-DIVORCE FINANCIAL PINCH

Essentially, the husband's obligation to his wife begins with marriage and terminates with divorce. Once divorced, the husband has no legal obligation to sustain his wife. They are separated, and both of them are on their own. In other words, divorce is a clean break.

But the situation is never so simple. Firstly, a woman left alone after divorce is in an extremely precarious position, and quite likely almost automatically becomes another statistic, living around the poverty level. On average, the wife's standard of living goes down 73% following divorce. On the other hand, the husband's living standard goes up 42%!

In the close-knit communities of yesteryear, with sensitivity to one another the prevailing norm, and social services for the poor well entrenched, this may not have been so serious a matter. Every poor person was a communal priority, and the divorced woman was included in that category. Indeed, some historians have been able to gauge the level of divorce within Jewish communities of yesteryear from the number of women on the poverty rolls.

~

TODAY'S REALITY

However, the social network of yesterday is not nearly as strong today. Additionally, the rate of divorce is so high, with the resulting number of divorced single women so extraordinarily large, that social networks alone will not address the problem. As a responsible community, we dare not let the woman go from the trauma of divorce to the travails of poverty.

All this does not begin to take into account the other overwhelming factor in the post-divorce financial quagmire, namely child support. When children are involved, the financial obligations of the husband to his ex-wife do not automatically terminate. True, the payments are in the form of support for expenses incurred in raising the children and providing for their education, but there is nevertheless direct and often painful financial dealing between the former spouses.

~

SETTLEMENT IN ISRAEL

Concerning the actual settlement of financial demands between husband and wife, the situation in Israel is different from that in the *golah* (outside Israel). Once a couple approaches the Rabbinical Court for divorce in Israel, the Rabbinical Court has jurisdiction in all of the nuances of the divorce, including finances and custody. Usually, the parties involved, or their spokespersons, will try to hammer out an agreement, often with the help of the presiding Rabbi of the Rabbinical Court.

The fact that the wife cannot be divorced against her will leaves her in a stronger position to demand some form of continuing support after marriage terminates.

This support could come in the form of regular payments, or in the form of one lump sum. It is not unusual that this lump sum is handed over to the court, with instruction that it is to be given to the wife only following the conclusion of the *get* procedure. This escrow arrangement would usually be the invoked procedure if there is ill-will between the couple, and mistrust that usually is an outgrowth of that ill-will.

~

MATRIMONIAL HOME

On occasion, the financial settlement prior to the finalization of the *get* may involve some arrangement concerning the matrimonial home, or other property. In such instance, the deeds office clerk may actually be summoned to the *Bet Din* to arrange that transfer right then and there.

The question of the matrimonial home is a matter of great importance and is not easily resolved. Generally, the person who owns the home, in whose name it has been registered either for ownership or rental, has the right to stay, and the other one must leave. That is the case if this becomes a contentious matter between the divorcing couple. They can, by agreement, override this consideration, and effectively work out some arrangement which is mutually acceptable to them.

Registration, however, is not the exclusive criterion via which ownership of the matrimonial home or other property is decided. A wife who is able to show that she paid for the matrimonial home or other property, even though it is registered in the husband's name, would likely be given that property. The reverse, however, is not the case. The husband who claims that he has ownership of the matrimonial home, even though it is in the wife's name, is in a weaker position.

Since it is more usual for the husband to give gifts to his wife, the fact that it is in her name is considered as evidence of his having given this to her as a gift, which she would retain after the divorce. However, it is not usual for a wife to give a gift, especially of that magnitude, to her husband. The fact that it is registered in the husband's name is not proof that the wife has given it to him as a gift, even though she has paid a significant part of the cost, if not all of it.

~

OTHER CONSIDERATIONS

When there are equal claims, the general tendency of the court is to lean in favor of the woman, that she remain in the matrimonial home. This is especially the case if there are children involved, and she is granted custody. The Rabbinical Court may also impose payments, in the form of compensation to the wife, especially in instances when there is no compelling reason for the husband to demand the divorce. They cannot point to any insubordination on the part of the wife that legitimizes his request. The court will use its good offices to compensate the woman as a trade-off for her cooperating in the granting of the *get*.

This is not an instance of blackmail or ransom. The court will not look favorably upon the woman using her right to refuse the *get* as a weapon with which to extract exorbitant sums from the husband. This she has no right to do, neither legally nor ethically. However, her request for some compensation to enable her to keep her head above water, and to not have anxieties about making ends meet, and on the assumption that the husband can afford these payments, is another matter altogether. Here the court would argue on her behalf.

It is self-evident that the wife is entitled to take out of the marriage all that she brought into it, namely any property or other possessions. The same would apply to gifts that were given to her by her husband during the marriage, as well as money she earned by herself, which by common agreement she kept as her own under a separate account.

~

TO AGREE OR NOT TO AGREE

Thus, in general, the financial arrangements for the divorcing couple fall into two categories: either mutually agreed upon, or imposed by the *Bet Din*. Insofar as husband and wife alone are concerned, they can agree to any arrangement following divorce which is mutually acceptable. The Rabbinical Court will in all likelihood endorse such an arrangement. The primary exception to this would be if their arrangement obviously disadvantages the children.

When there is no agreement between the couple, the Rabbinical Court must use its good offices to effect some equitable solution. Generally, the person who wants the divorce the most is the one who will probably have to give a little. However, the major consideration in settling matters is the welfare of the divorcing couple.

Much thought is given to the financial positions of both the husband and the wife, and their future possibilities for earning a living, as well as other factors, including their health and additional responsibilities. Also, the court as a general rule assures that the wife does not leave empty-handed. Aside from any compensation, it will give to her the furniture and other items that are necessary to maintain a household, especially if she is granted custody of the child or children.

~

PRIMARY OBLIGATION

Custody considerations aside, there is a general halakhic (Judeo-legal) convention that it is the father who has the obligation to maintain the child or children. Even though the technical, legal obligation for this only exists until the age of six, there is a further obligation following that age level, but that "obligation" is considered an act of charity by the father. This obligation is enforced till the age of 15, but should ideally be carried out until the child becomes self-sufficient.

The classic extolment of one who "performs charity at all times" is Talmudically applied to one who sustains his children when they are small (Ketuvot, 50a). Ostensibly this is a type of charity which would seem to be more obligatory than the general charity obligations of a communal nature. One who does not respond to every mail order charity envelope that is sent may not deserve community condemnation. But surely a father who refuses to provide for his children would be frowned upon by the general community.

~

SUSTENANCE AS CHARITY

Parenthetically, the idea that sustaining children after the age of six is only in the realm of charity has a logic of its own, much though this idea may startle the uninformed. Consider the not infrequent instances when children get into fights with their parents, and their parents throw back at the children their lack of

179

appreciation for all they have done for them. The children usually have at the ready a spontaneous retort, namely — "big deal, you had to do it anyway!"

Jewish law appropriately pulls the rug out from under the children in this regard. The parents can point out that after the age of six, the obligation to feed is an act of charity, rather than a strictly legal obligation. The children are thus told to appreciate that their parents were charitable with them, and they should therefore be charitable to their parents; if not with their finances, at least with their appreciation.

~

REASONABLENESS

Both husband and wife, as they untangle, and wrestle with the complicated matter of financial arrangements, should disavow, to their own selves, any thought of making a killing on the deal, or really "sticking it" to the other. Each has the obligation to do the right thing for the other, at the same time as they make sure that the other does the right thing by them. The one usually follows the other.

Granted that the finances are a matter of contention in divorce, as much as finances can be a matter of contention within marriage. Nevertheless, the basic thrust should be towards assuring financial security, and not toward punishing the other by imposing excessive, unreasonable, and unattainable demands. This creates ill-will and resistance. And from a practical point of view, it is self-defeating. It is understood that there will be many situations in which one of the couple thinks his or her request is reasonable, but the other thinks it to be an exorbitant demand. Through the good offices of an objective third party (in Israel that objective third party being the Rabbinical Court), these matters can be adjudicated in an impartial, objective, and mutually fair way.

The system may have its problems, but its general thrust, one of fairness and equity, should be applauded. One tends to hear only the negative. It is safe to say that the public at large is not aware of many of the guiding principles that govern the approach of the Rabbin-

ical Court in Israel. There are some bureaucratic problems. The Rabbinical Court is an
officially recognized legal authority, and does
get caught in the bureaucratic tangle that is
inimical to the entrenched system. The system
may move slowly, but the values of the system
are salutary.

~

AN UNUSED OPTION

The situation outside Israel is somewhat different than it is in Israel. The Jewish court
outside Israel has no jurisdictional power to
deal with divorce cases, aside from the purely
religious area of the transmission of the *get*.
Unlike in Israel, where once the Rabbinical
Court is approached, it has jurisdictional
powers over all components of the divorce,
outside Israel it is the secular courts which dictate what occurs in the divorce settlement. In
most instances, a couple will approach the
Rabbinical Court to finalize the Judaic side of
the separation only after all other outstanding
issues have been resolved, including the civil

divorce, the financial payment, and the custody settlement. It is unfortunate that couples who divorce do not think of the Rabbinical Court outside Israel as anything more than a religious court for religious matters. The idea that Rabbis should be involved in the final disposition of the matrimonial property and of custodial matters is quite foreign to most Jews.

This is lamentable, since generally, Jewish life does not make this type of arbitrary division between the religious and the ordinary. It refuses to evince concern only for the "religious," but not for the ordinary. Quite the contrary, the ordinary everyday dialectic is of vital importance in Judaism. The ordinary is itself potentially holy. The wide expanse of halakhic (Judeo-legal) literature on financial settlement in matrimonial matters, as well as the discussion of custody issues, is ample testimony to this.

~

RABBINICAL COURT'S POWER

But what legal standing could a Rabbinic decision on these matters have in a civil court? Quite a significant standing, if in fact this was an agreement that had been arranged with the parties involved, and their respective lawyers. Civil courts gladly welcome mediated agreement between the parties, for which they must just give their stamp of approval. As the courts are overloaded, the disputation associated with divorce is the type of painful and sometimes prolonged litigation most judges would love to avoid.

The matter of going to a civil court to extract greater payment, when there is questionable entitlement to this according to Jewish law, is an ethical issue of great import. Arguably, anyone who goes to a secular court to extract from that court what one is not entitled to according to Jewish law may in fact be guilty of stealing, of theft under the camouflage of secular or civil law. This is categorically forbidden.

Obviously, no amount of haranguing about

this will dissuade a member of the matrimonial union who is convinced that by going to a civil court he or she will get a much better deal than through mediation involving well-intentioned lawyers and Rabbis.

~

LOSING BY WINNING

It must be emphasized again, at the risk of reaching argumentum ad nauseam, that neither of the couple should go to a lawyer whose main objective is to win, to make as much money for the client, which at the same time of course makes that much more for the lawyer. The prospect of winning with a hot-shot lawyer is almost too inviting to resist. But the real question is — down the road who really wins?

By pummeling the other into submission through legal diatribe, you do win, but it is a pyrrhic victory. The victory comes at the price of burning all the bridges, of scorching the earth for future interaction, interaction which almost always remains if there are children involved.

Every spouse will have legitimate reason for pummelling the partner with a legal stick. There is no shortage of excuses to rationalize going into the bear pit, scratching and clawing for every single penny that may be available. But it creates a miserable atmosphere, an atmosphere in which the couple will be forced to live for the rest of their lives. It is an atmosphere which will likewise affect whatever new marriage is entered into, since the residue of bitterness will spill over, and even escalate. And of course, it is a bitter atmosphere which will adversely affect the children.

Then too, each one of the couple may swear up and down that he or she had the best of intentions to have an amicable settlement, but that it was the other one who ruined it all. The simple advice in the situation is—do not get caught in the blame game. Simply go about the business of doing the right thing in an ethically upright way.

Even if one gains a little bit less, in the end one will have gained in terms of peace of mind, in terms of being able to look at one's self in the mirror and say that you did the upright and proper thing. You and your posterity will be the better off for it. And that is worth the price.

~

EXPANDED RESPONSIBILITIES

Creating situations outside Israel whereby the Rabbinical Court works in conjunction with well-intentioned and settlement-oriented rather than gouging-oriented lawyers is a major step forward. It also places additional pressure on the Rabbinical Court system, which will need more competent people to handle the anticipated increased load.

However, there are more and more people who are learning the intricacies of Jewish law who can serve on these Rabbinical Courts. With expanding demand for Rabbis, there should come an increasing supply. There is no question that given the will to address the increasing spate of divorces, a way can be found.

Until that way is found, the situation

involving the divorcing couple will be less than
ideal. It is not unusual for a recalcitrant spouse
to use all the chips in the bargaining process
for a *get* to convince the other partner, usually
but not exclusively the wife, to waive some
claim that would have been justified in civil
court.

———

INEXCUSABLE CONDUCT

This bargaining is done through the victimized
spouse being cajoled or otherwise convinced
by the *Bet Din* that in the interests of finalizing the *get* process, they should waive some
financial consideration. Then there are some
outlandish and unforgivable incidents wherein
the recalcitrant husband, in order to become
cooperative in the granting of the divorce,
extorts exorbitant ransom money from the
wife or her family. All too often, this is done
with the tacit, if not overt approval of the
Rabbinical Court. This type of behavior, in
the process of fulfilling what is nothing less
than a *mitzvah*, a biblical mandate, is uncon-

scionable. It is particularly upsetting that precisely within the community which purports to observe God's law with meticulousness, that such extortion is resorted to for the fulfillment of what is a religious duty, namely to grant a divorce.

This outrage cannot be tolerated. No Rabbinical Court should in any way be involved in this type of negotiation, thereby giving credibility to extortion as a means of obtaining a *get*. Those same individuals who allow for this type of blackmail should instead weigh down quite heavily on the non-cooperating spouse, and resolutely warn that spouse about what consequences can be expected within the community for failure to cooperate.

As long as Rabbinical Courts outside Israel are perceived to be weak when it comes to taking up the cause of the oppressed, it will be well nigh impossible to suggest that Rabbis be used as mediators, or as consultants to mediation-oriented lawyers, for the purposes of amicably settling the financial issues of a divorce.

TO BE RESOLUTE

It is desirable that the couple who is divorcing seek the advice of the Rabbinical Court for the purposes of settling all outstanding issues, and for that settlement to be registered in the civil court via the lawyers. This will be achieved only if there is no equivocation concerning the basic and uncompromising adherence to fairness, equality, and compassion in the divorce process, free from threats and blackmail, or "green" mail.

There has been much talk of institutionalizing a pre-nuptial agreement, obligating the couple to obey the *Bet Din* with regard to the giving or accepting of the *get*. Though there is much to be said about this, suffice it to mention that the couple is already so obliged, by virtue of their being Jewish, and by virtue of marrying according to the Law of Moses and Israel. A pre-nuptial agreement will help the civil court to enforce the *get* procedure, but this itself is not without attendant problems. What is of undeniable importance is that the Rabbinical Courts stand up resolutely to their obligation to uphold the honor and dignity of the Torah, through unswerving adherence to Jewish law and ethics.

~

MAKING THE KETUBAH POTENT

Additionally, the *ketubah* document, which is so crucial in Israel, should perhaps be reexamined, in terms of it becoming more than just a pro forma document with no real teeth.

As mentioned previously, in Israel there is an additional clause within the *ketubah* which addresses the specific situation of the husband and wife who are getting married. The undertaking written within the *ketubah* is for a settlement at the termination of marriage, significantly above what would normally accrue from the *ketubah*.

This same type of arrangement could easily be transferred to marriages outside Israel. This need not even entail a specific undertaking of a precise amount, or a lump sum that the husband agrees to pay the wife upon termination of the marriage.

The clause could simply read that "the husband also takes upon himself to provide appropriate support payments for the wife and children, should the marriage dissolve, as is prescribed by the Rabbinical Court mutually agreed to by the couple."

This type of protection within the *ketubah* will give the woman in marriage much greater confidence to entrust the Rabbinical Court with playing a key role in the final disposition of the marital property, and as well in adjudicating custodial arrangements.

~

FACING REALITY

With divorce increasingly becoming a fact of life within the Jewish community, and unfortunately so, it is silly to deny this reality, and not face up to it with the full energies that the situation demands. By taking preemptive steps, we will be able to establish a new climate of appreciation for the Judaic way in divorce, which will be beneficial to the divorcing spouses, their progeny, the larger family, and the entire Jewish community. To do anything less would be to abdicate responsibility in this most serious, contentious, and explosively divisive issue.

Chapter 12
CUSTODY CONSIDERATIONS

~

SOLOMONIC WISDOM

Perhaps the most contentious issue in the finalization of a divorce is the matter of who gains
custody of the children, and the attendant visitation rights for the one to whom custody has
not been granted.

It is in the matter of custody that most con-
flicts arise, most tug-pulling takes place, and
the most serious consequences endure. A telling episode involving King Solomon is quite
instructive for custody battles.

That story concerns the famous conflict
between two mothers. Each of the mothers
had given birth, but one of those newborns

died. There being two mothers with only one surviving newborn, each mother claimed that the surviving child was hers.

No one knew how to establish whose claim was the correct one, and the case came before King Solomon. Having heard the claims of the two parents, he too apparently could not decide, and ordered that the baby be cut into two. Each one of the parents would be given one-half of the child. Normally, in an equal claims situation involving property, a fifty-fifty split may be the appropriate settlement if no one has overwhelming arguments, and there are no squatter's rights involved, or no one is holding title.

However, when a baby is split fifty-fifty, neither mother has a child. But this was King Solomon's decision, and he then awaited the reaction of the two mothers. One mother said that this was a fair judgment, since each one would be given an equal portion, and no mother would have more than the other. The other mother could not accept this verdict, and insisted she would rather let the other one have the child, just do not kill it.

~

THE DECISION

When King Solomon heard this, he immediately said that the lady who did not want the baby split fifty-fifty is the true mother. She was awarded "custody" of the child (I Kings, 3:16–27).

One can conjecture that a true mother would not want her child to be killed, and the fact that one "mother" said that this was a fair solution was proof this was not really her child.

On the other hand, it is also possible that the woman who agreed to the child being cut in two may have been the biological mother, but her own selfish considerations, and whatever rivalry she may have had with the other contending mother, allowed her to place personal victory over the welfare of the child. It is conceivable that she was the biological mother, but in the judgment of King Solomon was unfit to be a real life mother. The other woman, who may not have been the biological mother of the child, but whose feelings for the child overwhelmed any other personal considerations, was deemed to be the appropriate custodian for the child.

~

REMOVE EGO

This entire episode is instructive for custody situations, since it is here that parents are locked into an "ego vs. welfare-of-the-child" conflict. Each one of the divorcing parents may want to have the child to him- or herself, but in the process, the child may get chopped into pieces. True parenthood is here realized by both parents placing their egos far into the background, removing the child or the children from the battlefield, the arena of their conflict. In a self-transcending manner, they do what is best for the child. Sometimes, doing the best for the child means giving up on what the parents may perceive to be their right.

~

BEYOND RIGHTS

Insofar as the issue of rights in the matter of custody is concerned, it should be noted that within the Judaic ethical sphere, rights do not come into question. We speak in Jewish ethics of responsibilities that one has to one's self, to others within society, and to God.

The fundamental principles of Judaic ethics involve our responsibility for the welfare of others. Even the recipients of our concern do not have a right to them. The poor person, for example, does not have the right to take money out of the rich person's pocket. However, the rich person does have an obligation to give charity to the poor.

Aside from the legal parameters of ethical responsibilities as spelled out in Jewish law, there are extra-legal categories, such as: our behavior should emulate the way of the pious (Talmud, Shabbat, 120a); we should be governed by a higher ethic, namely to please God with our behavior (ibid.); we should do that which is upright and correct (Deuteronomy, 6:18); and we should go in the way of good

people (Proverbs, 2:20). These are ethical for-
mulations which should govern the way we
behave under all circumstances.

———

THE PRIMARY CONCERN

With special regard to the parent-child dialectic, the parents do not have rights over their
children. They have responsibilities towards
their children, even as the children, as they
enter into the age of responsibleness, then
become obligated in fulfilling their duties
towards their parents.

The governing principle in deciding the custody of the children is not what is the right of
the parent, or parents, but what is right for
the child.

Civil courts in general do gravitate towards
the welfare of the child as being a primary
concern, if not the primary concern. But the
rights of the parents, specifically the non-
custodial parents, are at least somewhat taken
into account. Within Jewish law, the question
of rights does not enter into the picture. The

focus is exclusively on the good of the child. Whatever is good for the child then becomes incorporated as the general guideline for how the divorcing parents will have their responsibilities apportioned.

—

IMPACT ON CHILDREN

It is important for divorcing parents to realize that their divorce can have a devastating effect on their children, potentially even more serious than the death of a parent. The children can be caught up in the continuing conflict with the parents, and may even become pawns in this dragged-out battle. The effects of this on the child can be nothing short of disastrous. They will see themselves as locked into a trauma with no exit. This may cause them to become frustrated, depressed, and even permanently melancholic.

Parents can help lighten the children's burden by resolving not to allow whatever animosity that may exist between them to spill over to the children. Indeed this is difficult, but if the resolve is there, and the parents, instead of imposing this ethic on the other, each imposes it on him- or herself, a relatively peaceful environment is more likely to unfold.

Part of the devastation associated with a divorce is the illogical but nevertheless real feeling children have, that they may be at fault, or even the cause of the separation. It is important for the parents to be wise enough, and mature enough, to disabuse the children of this. They must also assure them that no matter what difficulties they may be having together as spouses, they still love the children, and that love will be unaffected by the divorce. This message is best conveyed by the parents together sitting down with all the children.

~

JOINT CUSTODY

No matter what custody arrangement is finalized, the only way it will work, with minimal long lasting damage to the child or children, is with the full cooperation of the parents. Parents may go into the custody component of their divorce with each one wanting to be the winner of the custody battle, but this can never work. There can be no situation when both of them will be the winners.

Even a joint custody arrangement does not necessarily make both of them winners, by virtue of the fact that neither of them has lost entirely, or gained an advantage over the other. Even though joint custody seems to have become more popular in the present day, it is still not abundantly clear that this is the best way for child care following divorce to be finalized. Joint custody works only with children who can cope with the arrangement, when there is enough money for the support of two households, when the two homes are not too far apart, and when there is a firm commitment to the arrangement by both the parents, with the attendant flexibility if there are unforeseen circumstances which demand adjustment.

The major argument against joint custody is that when the child oscillates between two homes, it really has no home. This is a crucial matter. It is crucial because having a strong home is basic to the child's development. When there is a separation, it may be in the best interests of the child to have one solid home, and another place which the child visits occasionally, but which is not home, much as the child would go to another relative or friend for an overnight or two.

~

JEWISH PERSPECTIVE

As with financial matters, when the divorce takes place outside Israel, the issue of custody is unfortunately not usually settled within the parameters of Judaic law. The ultimate jurisdiction for custody resides with the civil courts. These courts obviously go along with whatever arrangement has been made between the husband and wife, and finalized through their lawyers, provided that this agreement is not of obvious detriment to the child or children involved.

In Israel, once a couple approaches the *Bet*

Din for divorce, the custody arrangements will be incorporated in the finalization of the *get*.

From a Judaic perspective, it is obviously preferable that the issue of custody, like the issue of finances, is handled within the parameters of Jewish law. Even outside Israel, this is achievable if the couple resorts to the more amicable process of working things out between themselves, with the help of Rabbis whom they trust, and with the couple's legal representatives, provided that these lawyers are themselves more interested in resolution than in protracted conflict.

~

CRUCIAL MATTER

Every child needs maternal nurturing and paternal guidance. In the general population, only one-fifth of children from a divorced parental set maintain good relations with both parents. About three-fifths have a good relationship with the mother, and one-third have a good relationship with the father. One-third never see one of the parents.

Not surprisingly, half of all divorcing couples fight over parental sharing. The children are caught in the middle, and denied the stability and parenting that they deserve. The stakes are high, and the responsibility great. The parents must agree to agree.

~

GENERAL RULE

The general principle by which the Rabbinical Court operates is that for children up to age six, whether boys or girls, custody is given to the mother.

For children over the age of six, the sons would generally be placed in the custody of the father, since he has the primary obligation to educate the child and to raise the child as a Jew. The daughters are generally placed with their mothers, since the daughters will become better educated in the ways in life that are indigenous to them through the more intimate relationship they would have with their mothers.

As an aside, it is interesting to note that the

general societal pattern with regard to children of divorced parents is that girls do best with their mothers after divorce, and boys do equally well with their mothers or fathers. The considerations which govern this general Judaic rule are uncannily consistent with psychological wisdom. However, even if psychological wisdom did not generally correlate with the Judaic principles of custody, these principles would still be operative.

―――

PSYCHOLOGICAL CONSIDERATIONS

Still, Rabbinical Courts do take into account the views of psychologists concerning specific situations. However, they will be very careful about the nature of the advice that is given. If psychologists will argue for a different custody arrangement than is the normal practice, because they feel that in general this is preferable, the Rabbis will likely reject such advice. Thus, for example, if the psychologist suggests that in general it is better for a boy of the age of nine to be with his mother, the Rabbinical Court will discount this advice.

However, if the psychologist comes with a recommendation based on a particular understanding of this unique situation, and that recommendation runs contrary to the normal practice, this is a different matter. If a psychologist argues that in this particular situation, the nine year old boy is better off with the mother because he has an estranged relationship with his father, or because the father is not psychologically equipped to care for the child on his own, the court would take this opinion very seriously. It is the welfare of the child that is of paramount importance, within the context of the general framework as it has been spelled out in Jewish law.

~

DIFFERENT CIRCUMSTANCES

These general guidelines, of the child until six going to the mother, and after six going to the same-sex parent, are all subject to change based on circumstance. Thus, an obviously unfit mother who beats the child, or who is habitually drunk, or is mentally unstable, could not claim legal right to custody. The court may in such instances decide against leaving the child with the mother, even if it is below the age of six.

Additionally, when even casual, intermittent contact with either of the parents is considered to be deleterious to the child's welfare, the Rabbinical Court may in fact prohibit such visitation by the abusing or unfit parent. Visitation of the children comes under the same rubric as custody itself; it is looked upon as the child's right, not the parent's right. When it is deemed to be in the best interests of the child, then it is a part of the long range agreement. When it is detrimental to the child, then visitation is curtailed.

Because visitation is a right of the child, the fact that the parent who is obligated to pay support, the father, is derelict in such support payments, would not be cause to deny the father the visitation to the child. Were this a right that were granted to the father, then one could speak of the father forfeiting that right for failure to live up to his responsibilities.

However, since this is the child's right, the father's dereliction with regard to support cannot be employed as just cause for denying the child that which the child needs; i.e., contact with the father.

~

THE CHILD'S WELFARE

The Rabbinical Court will look upon all components of the children's welfare in making its custody decision, if in Israel, or its custody recommendation, if outside Israel. This will include the mental stability of the parents, and the importance of all the children remaining together under one roof.

Also included in the concern for the children's welfare will be the children's spiritual growth. Thus, if one of the parents will refuse to raise the children in a Jewish environment, and will refuse to give the children a Jewish education, this will weigh heavily in the court's decision.

This can lead to the very unlikely scenario of a court deciding that both parents may be unfit. For example, if both parents, for whatever reason, decided to leave the Jewish fold, and entrusting the children to either of the parents will almost guarantee that the children's Jewish identity will be lost, the court can recommend that the children be given over to a third party.

This third party could be an orphanage which raises children responsibly. Or, in situations when this is possible, it could be grandparents who are ready, willing, and able to assume full responsibility for the children's welfare. These are options that may be entertained by the Rabbinical Court when the situation is of such gravity that radical custody arrangements are the only options beneficial to the child.

Not only spiritual matters may lead to such decisions of the Rabbinical Court. If the Rabbinical Court becomes aware that both parents are child abusers, and beat the children, they will likely deny custody to any abusing parent. Custody would be awarded to a third party.

~

PARENTAL AGREEMENTS

The parents may ideally decide on a custody arrangement for their children, which as mentioned before would be looked upon favorably by the court. However, if in its opinion the joint arrangement made by the parents is not in the children's best interests, the Rabbinical Court may decide against endorsing such an agreement. If, for example, the arrangement includes the mother's agreement that the daughter will stay with the father, the court may reject this. It is not the mother's right which she can then give up to the father; it is the right of the child to be raised with her mother, over which the mother has no right. She may legitimately claim incompetence, or lack of strength to do her duty, but she cannot arbitrarily give her daughter away.

Custody matters can never be a barter in the combat between husband and wife. Thus, the woman who buys off her husband's recalcitrance by promising to allow him custody of a child over whom she would normally have been given custody, will not be disadvantaged by such actions. The *get* may then be given by the husband, but the Rabbinical Court will reject out of hand any prior agreement which was the basis for the granting of the divorce. It will award custody based on what is in the best interests of the child, the prior parental agreement notwithstanding.

~

CHILD'S PREFERENCE

The child is consulted, if the child is mature enough to have authentic feelings, not planted ones. With obvious exception, the mature assertion of a child that it desires to be with a certain parent would be given overriding importance. Thus, a boy aged eleven or twelve who states unequivocally that he wants to be with his mother, and not with his father, would be granted this wish, even though this is contrary to the general principle that boys go with the father.

The Rabbinical Court operates under the general principle that the notion of the best interests of the child can hardly be carried out if the child expressly states that he does not want a certain arrangement. And, in a more positive vein, the child's expressed desire to live with a certain parent is more likely to correlate with the child's best interests, unless there is clear evidence to the contrary. The child does not make the decision, but the child's choice weighs very heavily in the ultimate decision.

VISITATION RESPONSIBILITIES

Once that decision is made, and custody is awarded to one of the parents, the other parent is usually accorded "visitation responsibilities." We are normally accustomed to call these visitation rights; but they are not rights, they are responsibilities.

The fact that a couple divorces does not mean that their responsibilities to their children have been diminished. They are both obligated to assure that their children grow up to be upright, respectful, well-balanced individuals. Heretofore, it was a collective effort under one roof. Now, it is a joint effort under separate roofs, but nevertheless an endeavor to which they must both be uncompromisingly committed.

There are ongoing horror stories, or at the very least complaints, that one hears from the non-custodial parent. These are that the visitation always involves hassles, that the custodial parent does not cooperate in making the visitation as amicable and tranquil as it could be and should be. This is unfortunate, truly most unfortunate for the child or children.

Whoever it is that is granted custody should not see him- or herself as the victor, but rather as the one who has primary responsibility. The custodial parent, through the order of the Rabbinical Court, has the primary responsibility to raise the child. This primary responsibility also includes the sacred obligation to maintain a pleasant atmosphere under all circumstances, including the time for the non-custodial parent's visitation. That the non-custodial parent comes to visit is the right of the child, and no parent has a right to compromise on what belongs to the child by rights.

The visitation itself should be a meaningful

endeavor. The visiting parent must resist the temptation to do so much in so little time. Particularly should the visiting parent avoid the all too inviting opportunity to spoil the child with good times and lavish treats. This is only a temporary pacifier. It does not build relationships. It also creates unfair comparisons in the child's mind, between the disciplining but concerned custodial parent, and the wildly generous but frivolous visiting parent.

KEEPING THE PEACE

It is the height of irresponsibility for any parent to incite a child against the other parent. The obligation of children to honor their parents is an imperative which is best realized through the parents creating the environment which would lead to the children respecting them. The greatest challenge in this regard comes when the parents are divorced. They are now separated, but they share collectively the responsibility to encourage the children's respecting them. Either of the parents who incites the children against the other parent is in breach of this most serious parental responsibility, and thereby places an enormous stumbling block in front of the children.

It would be also wise for any embittered and vindictive parent to realize that by setting the child against the other parent, he or she may temporarily win the battle, but down the road will lose the war. The child may go along with parental machinations, but only because the child is captive to the custodial parent.

Any normal child will harbor a strong resentment against a parent who places him or her in the uncomfortable position of having to reject the other parent. Because, under normal circumstances, a child wants to have both a father and a mother. It was only by parental decision to divorce that the father and the mother are not together, but divorce is not legitimate reason for either of the parents to deny the child access to the other parent.

~

THE REAL WINNERS

A parent who wants to be a winner in the custody battle can best achieve this by placing any personal vendetta aside, and doing the best to encourage the child's ongoing, positive relationship with the non-custodial parent. No words of a negative nature about the other parent should ever be uttered by the custodial parent.

Obviously, the same is true of the visiting parent, who should likewise refrain from any negative comments about the custodial parent. Each of the parents should assume that the other will try to do the best in their role. If they do not, then it is something that is to be worked out between them. The child should not be brought into the picture as a combatant in the conflict.

~

CHILD SUPPORT

Whilst the matter of who gains custody of the child is to be determined by the court, based on general principles, and the exceptional circumstances that may prevail in specific situations, the matter of child support is much more straightforward. As a general rule, it is the obligation of the father to support the children.

This obligation of the father to support the children is independent of any custody arrangements. Thus, even if the court decides that it is in the best interests of the children to remain with the mother, the obligation of the father to maintain the children remains unchanged and unabated. He must support the children even if he is not the custodial parent.

~

WITHHOLDING SUPPORT

The father does have the right to withhold maintenance payments for the children, if their not being with him goes against the expressed wishes of the Rabbinical Court. Thus, a son, who under normal circumstances would after the age of six go to the father, may refuse to leave the mother. In this instance the father can withhold payment until the child joins him. The same is true of a daughter who should, according to the decision of the court, go to her father for whatever reason. If she refuses, the father can withhold maintenance.

This is not to suggest that the father should withhold maintenance; it is only to state that the father cannot be forced into a maintenance obligation when the custodial arrangement is inconsistent with the expressed wishes of the *Bet Din*. The father may say that unless and until the child joins him, as per the court's custodial decision, he will not assume maintenance responsibilities. He is not obliged to support a reality which is inconsistent with the decision of the *Bet Din*.

THE CHILD'S RIGHT

Barring that circumstance, the father's obligation for the maintenance of the children is clear-cut. Generally, that obligation is basic until the age of six. After six, it is, as previously pointed out, in the category of charity that the father is obligated to provide for the children. Generally, this "charity" is expected of the father at least until the children have reached the age of fifteen, but ideally until the children are self-sufficient.

The parents would be well advised to work out the financial arrangements between themselves. This is the best case scenario for all components of the divorce settlement, including maintenance. However, maintenance agreements are always subject to the overriding question of whether it is in the best interests of the children. No waiver of responsibility that is given by the mother, for whatever consideration, can be implemented if it is harmful to the child or children.

Any agreement the mother may have made with the father that, in trade-off for his agreement to grant the *get*, she will not demand child support, is irrelevant insofar as the children are concerned. The father's obligation to maintain the children is not a back door obligation that is channelled through the mother. It is a direct obligation of the father to his children, and therefore the mother has no right to compromise the children's interests. A Rabbinical Court to whom it is obvious that the divorcing parents' agreement will create severe economic hardships for the children, will reject such agreement, and will assure that the children are given the proper resources necessary for their growth and development.

―――

NO FAULT MAINTENANCE

As with the custody matter itself, maintenance arrangements are contemplated irrespective of the responsibility that the wife may have for the break-up of the marriage. It may be that she is directly responsible, through her dereliction, for the marriage disintegrating. It may even be that the responsibility is so great that she is denied the *ketubah* settlement. This, however, does not by definition lead to her not having custody, or being denied maintenance. The question of custody is based on what is in the best interests of the child. It is quite possible that in spite of all that had transpired, it is in the best interests of the child to be with the mother.

Once that is the decision, indeed whatever the decision, the child is entitled to full maintenance. The exact amount given for maintenance takes into account various factors. These include the needs of the children, both for food, shelter, and clothing, and as well for education. It also includes the attention that the children need. This attention given by the mother to the children is of the type which entitles her to some compensation.

The court will weigh quite seriously the fact that the mother has decided to forego any work which would compromise the time she has for her children, and instead intends to devote full time and attention to the children. This too falls under the rubric of maintenance. Depending on the specific needs and costs involved, this would be incorporated in whatever maintenance charges are to be assumed by the father.

~

LATER CHANGES

Whatever arrangements have been finalized through the Rabbinical Court can be changed later on, if it becomes obvious that the situation has changed dramatically, and the best interests of the children are at stake. For example, if the custody of the son had been awarded to the father, but the father then proceeds to marry out of the faith, this would be reason enough for the Rabbinical Court to reexamine its initial decision, and place the child in the care of the mother.

This is not a punishment to the intermarrying parent. It is an affirmation of the *Bet Din's* concern for the long range spiritual welfare of the child, who deserves to grow up in a Jewish environment.

It is helpful in the long run for the parties who divorce to appreciate that whatever decision was made and implemented can be undone if the parents do not live up to their responsibilities. This is certainly the case if the custodial parent is obviously derelict. The realization that misbehavior, or parental delinquency, can result in the Rabbinical Court reexamining its decision, will hopefully serve as a prod to exercise responsibility with utmost seriousness and care, such that reexamination of the original decision will not be necessary.

~

MAKING BEST OF NEW REALITY

For the parents who must now live with the decision of the Rabbinical Court, their obligation is to make the best of the circumstances. They may have misgivings, even continual complaints about the court decision, which did not conform with their desires. But they must at all costs set this aside, and concentrate on doing the best, within the constraints placed upon them, to enhance the welfare of their children.

The visiting parent should assume that the custodial parent will try to do the best possible under the circumstances.

The custodial parent should realize that the visiting parent will be significantly pained by the complications involved in having to now go out of the way to experience what previously came naturally. It is not natural for a parent to continually come knocking on a door, to pick up the child, take the child away, and then bring the child back.

This is likewise also difficult for the child. But all difficulties can be made much more manageable with the cooperation of all involved. It helps for the custodial parent to realize that the visitation of the other parent is a right of the child. No parent would want to be accused of standing in the way of denying the child that which belongs to the child.

Even though there is no husband/wife connection, the parents do have a common interest in the welfare of the children. They should therefore have a reciprocal appreciation for what is done by the other in the children's best interest. The Judaic obligation to acknowledge the good that is done by others (*hakarat hatov*), applies even when one may have grievances against that party.

~

MOVING AWAY

At no point in time should the custodial parent contemplate a move away from the present locale, for the express purpose of distancing the child from the visiting parent. Using personal animus as a basis for depriving the child of the parent which it already sees only on a limited basis, is not the proper way to behave.

In instances when the parent does so disadvantage the child by moving, the Rabbinical Court may very well deprive the custodial parent of the custody. On the other hand, there must be legitimate reason for the move, and an obvious advantage to the child, which justifies the child's being denied the visitation of the non-custodial parent.

~

MOVING TO ISRAEL

One such instance when this type of move may actually be contemplated, is if the custodial parent desires to move to Israel with the child.

It is generally acknowledged that a child who is raised in Israel will have a much healthier and stronger sense of Jewishness. A move of this nature is thus normally deemed to be in the best interests of the child. Even here, whatever move is contemplated should be made with the child in mind, and not for the purpose of getting back at the other. It should also only be done after consultation with the Rabbinical Court, and after having gained its approval.

Insofar as moving to Israel is concerned, this can also be a weighty factor in the original dispensation of the Rabbinical Court. Thus, the Rabbinical Court, which is normally inclined to granting custody of a daughter to its mother, may think otherwise if the father expresses a desire to, or already resides in Israel, and would have the daughter living with him in Israel. Israel is such a positive ingredient in the child's development that it may change the normal pattern of custodial judgment by the Rabbinical Court.

In such instances, Rabbinical Courts have been known to judge on occasion for the father in Israel, and on other occasions for the mother outside Israel. With all the clear-cut guidelines, each individual case must be treated on its own merits. Many factors, including the locale of the parents, the parents' own personal commitment, the nature of the parents' relationship with the child, the child's own feelings, and the independent assessment of experts in child development, all will be taken into the equation. The final decision of the Rabbinical Court is therefore an enlightened one. It is one with which the divorcing parents should feel comfortable, even if either or both of them do not get their way.

~

THE REAL IMPLEMENTERS

The bottom line in all the custodial decisions made by the Rabbinical Court is that whilst the Rabbinical Court may make the decision, the key element is its implementation. There is no police force in the world that can monitor parental behavior to the last iota. And, even if it could monitor the overt behavior, it cannot monitor the hidden thoughts, the innuendos, the snide remarks, all those factors which create either a positive or a negative atmosphere.

All this is purely in the hands of the parents. It is they who, through the way they handle the situation, will make or break their posterity. They, by the nature of their commitment, and the ethical posture with which they carry it out, are the real implementers of the Court's decision.

Chapter 13
AFTERMATH PROTOCOL

~

TALMUDIC DIVORCE

What is the fundamental nature of the relationship between the husband and wife who have divorced? One would normally think that if there were no children born to the couple during the marriage, that after they have split, and all outstanding issues have been resolved, they are to each other as total strangers. However, this is not the case.

The nature of the post-divorce protocol between husband and wife is best spelled out in an episode that is reported in the Jerusalem Talmud (Ketuvot, 11:3), and also in the Midrash (Leviticus Rabbah, 34:14). It concerns a Talmudic sage by the name of Rabbe Yose, whose life was made miserable by his wife. After enduring continued hardship, but with much agonizing, he divorced his wife.

The wife remarried, but regrettably the fortunes of Rabbe Yose's ex-wife and her new husband fell dramatically and precipitously. The new husband lost his vision, and had to be led by his wife as they went from neighborhood to neighborhood to beg for alms.

The wife was understandably reluctant to venture into the neighborhood of her ex-husband, Rabbe Yose. The new husband, upon perceiving this reluctance, actually began to beat his wife in public. This scene caused a great furor, and no end of embarrassment to Rabbe Yose's ex-wife. By chance, Rabbe Yose saw this scene unfolding. He immediately took his ex-wife and her husband, and placed them in a residence to which he had access. He also brought provisions to sustain them for the remainder of their lives.

~

BEYOND THE LEGAL

Rabbe Yose was under no strictly legal obligation to behave as he did. But, as is made clear
in both the Talmud and the Midrash, he was
living through the ideal form of post-divorce
protocol, which urges the divorcing couple not
to be oblivious to their own flesh. The Talmud
states that the obligation, "and do not be
oblivious to your own flesh" (Jeremiah, 58:7),
applies specifically to the wife whom one has
divorced.

When the husband and wife were married,
they were considered as one. Since they were
united symbolically, spiritually, even physically, as one corpus, they are forever linked
through that original union. The divorce may
separate them, but the linkage of flesh which
once existed does not automatically evaporate
into nothingness. It remains forever.

Thus, the ethical application of the obligation to be mindful of one's own flesh, or as it is
expressed in the prohibitive, not to be oblivious to one's own flesh, is applied to that very
flesh and blood relationship which one may,

under normal circumstances, perceive as having terminated. It has not terminated, and the
relationship goes on.

~

ALWAYS LINKED

The ethical imperative, "be not oblivious to
your own flesh," is applied to the spouse whom
one has divorced. One could ask the simple
question — why apply it to the ex-mate, and
not to the more obvious flesh and blood relationships, such as one's grandchildren, or cousins, or whomever?

This obligation, not to neglect one's own
flesh, is the culmination of a verse extolling the
virtues of authentic charity. It could hardly be
a great virtue that you give charity to your
own flesh and blood; certainly not a culminat-
ing virtue, over and above those cited at the
beginning of the verse, namely bringing unre-
lated poor people into the home, and covering
those who are unclothed. This is something
which people do under normal circumstances,
and is not even considered anything extraordi-

nary. People normally do fend for others within the family.

Thus, one is left with no other choice but to understand this imperative as referring to an extraordinary situation, wherein there is a flesh and blood relationship, but the nature of that relationship is such that one would normally not expect that any obligation for support still exists.

Accordingly, this imperative is applied to none other than the spouse whom you have divorced, who once and therefore always is your own flesh and blood. Even though convention may absolve one from any obligations to a former spouse, Judaic ethical principles do not allow for such release.

~

CONTINUAL COMPASSION

Thus, the obligation to give of one's income to charity is applied to one's ex-wife. If one's ex-wife has sunk into poverty, then the ex-

234

husband should give of his charity allotment to his ex-wife. She has priority over all other poor.

This dictum certainly comes as a surprise, since it flies in the face of what would normally be the post-divorce pattern. One can see in this moral prescription an instructive message with regard to the husband and wife after divorce; that they still have obligations to each other. Even though the relationship has obviously changed, there is nevertheless an ongoing connection, and therefore an ongoing moral and ethical responsibility.

By being mindful of the obligation to exercise this responsibility should it become necessary, the divorcing couple is made aware that whereas the marital relationship may have been characterized by the passion of each for the other, the post-divorce situation should at the very least be characterized by the presence of compassion of each for the other.

This is nothing less than ethical programming, consistent with the spirit of the Torah, which urges individuals to conquer innate desires, to rise above petty, vindictive behavior; especially in circumstances when one might be likely to wallow in such negative expression.

———

THE FUNDAMENTAL PRINCIPLE

This, then, is the fundamental principle of the aftermath protocol; that there is an ongoing connection between husband and wife, even without the presence of children. This is a connection which places upon the divorcing husband primarily, the obligation to at all times have compassion for his ex-wife, and to assure that she never sinks into poverty and despair. Husbands who have divorced their wives may wish the worst for their ex-partners, and would love to gloat over their total failure. But that cannot be the Jewish way, and should not be allowed to become the Jewish way.

———

COOPERATION

If the divorcing couple were blessed with children during their marriage, then the divorce

takes on an added dimension of ongoing con-
nectedness, via the children. Like it or not, the
husband and wife will thereby be involved
with each other on an ongoing basis. They will
hopefully discuss such matters as the children's
education, the children's general welfare,
their health, their summer camp schedule, the
visitation procedures, and adjustments of the
custodial arrangements when one or the other
of the divorcing mates may have difficulty
keeping to the usual pattern.

If compassion and understanding are the
fundamental ethics of the post-divorce situation between the couple, then goodwill and
cooperation should be the governing ethics of
the husband and wife when it concerns the
welfare of the children.

~

GUARANTEED DELIVERY

Both husband and wife should be aware that
whatever they tell their children will be
relayed to the other spouse. It may not be done
with precision, but the general tenor of the

remarks made by one of the ex-mates about the other will find its way back to the original object of the remarks.

Thus, if a custodial mother complains about the fact that the visiting father is nasty, or does not really care about the child, or was always a rotten husband, her remarks will find their way back to the visiting father. One need not have a vivid imagination to picture what type of down-side syndrome this will initiate.

The father who hears that he has been bad-mouthed by his ex-wife will most probably become furious at her (if he is not already). He might also at the same time launch a counter-attack, by badmouthing his ex-wife to his child or children. This negative rhetoric is also likely to follow in a reverse type of custody, with the father the custodial parent and the mother the visiting parent.

The child is inevitably dragged into this ongoing conflict, and may become the carrier pigeon for the invective, as well as the ultimate victim of the long-range missiles hurled by the ex-mates at each other. The ongoing ill-will between the former spouses may result in a renewed court challenge to the original arrangement. Or worse, it may result in the custodial parent shutting the door to the visiting parent, or in the visiting parent taking the child on a designated visiting week-end and disappearing to another locale, even another country. This is the tragic scenario that can result from ill-will, and the unsavory remarks made by the spouses about each other.

~

RELAYING THE GOOD

On the other hand, consider the scenario in which each one of the couple resolves to say only nice things about the ex-mate. This may be hard to swallow originally, at the onset of divorce, but the rewards are well worth it. Each one of the divorcing couple would probably be well advised to rehearse within himself or herself such statements as — you know that your father really loves you; or, I really appreciate the extraordinary steps your father is taking to make sure that he sees you as often as possible; or, you have a very caring mother;

or, your mother is really going out of her way to do the best for you.

The more you rehearse these comments, the easier it will be to say them. The effect of these positive comments about your ex-mate can be of never-ending benefit. On the undeniable assumption that whatever you say about your former partner will be carried back to him or her, the nice comments that are made will engender a good feeling by the former spouse, who probably expects just the opposite.

The ex-mate who hears that nice things are said about him or her will in turn more likely say nice things about the other to the child. The child will then once again be a carrier pigeon, the carrier of good words, and will thereby be the elicitor of good feelings between the ex-spouses. Most importantly, the negative impact of divorce on the children may thereby be checked.

The cooperative spirit this can establish will be of benefit not only to the child, but also to the divorcing couple. They will remove the agenda of bitterness from each other, and get on with life in a positive way.

———

ANGER SELF-DESTRUCTIVE

No matter how much one may deny it, by being bitter towards the other and ventilating one's anger at the other, one does not thereby get rid of it. One is actually rehearsing that anger within the self. The anger will remain, and quite likely intensify.

The biblical advice, to "eliminate anger from your heart" (Ecclesiastes, 11:10), is most appropriate to a divorcing couple. For it is they who are more likely to have anger in their heart, and therefore it is they who must remove it. With bitterness in the heart, one is not likely to find peace of mind.

The biblical phrase, "and eliminate anger from your heart," is followed by the words, "and remove evil from your flesh." Indeed, by eliminating anger, you remove evil from your flesh. "Your flesh" may refer to one's own flesh, or to one's spouse, who once and always is as one's flesh. By taking away anger, one removes the potential for a harmful post-divorce relationship.

Maintaining anger will also stand in the

way of the embittered spouse linking with another partner. No individual would like to become entangled with a partner who, however attractive as a potential mate, is full of anger, hostility, and bitterness. That is sure to cloud any future relationship, or more probably, forestall the possibility of such a relationship ever developing.

~

THE BIBLICAL BASE

It is so obvious that the high road, the road of rising above the circumstances and behaving with understanding and goodwill, is the way to adopt. The basis for this is the biblical obligation to "love your neighbor as yourself . . . " (Leviticus, 19:18). According to Maimonides, this ethical charge is fulfilled through saying nice things about others. We would love others to say nice things about ourselves. To love others as ourselves means to do for them what you would want them to do for you. Uttering words of praise for your former spouse is a fulfillment of this most all-embracing Torah commandment.

The biblical basis for this goodwill approach is reinforced via the positive results that would ensue. No matter how illogical it may seem, no matter how outlandish it may appear, no matter how out-of-tune it may be with what normally happens after divorce, the superiority of the high-road approach must be hammered home with unabating force, as being *the* Jewish way of reacting in the post-divorce situation.

———

TO DEMAND OF ONE'S SELF

But it is the way that is not to be demanded by each of the spouses from the other. It is the way that each of the spouses should demand of his or herself. Neither of them should wait until the other makes the first move towards saying nice things. If either one waits for the other, it will be a long wait. Each should assume the responsibility to initiate the kind statements, the understanding words, the positive comments about the other.

Words can injure, words can heal. There has been enough injury to the home through the disruption of divorce. What the children, and indeed the divorcing couple, do not need in the post-divorce situation is further injury. What they do need is healing. And there is no better healing than kind words that emanate from the mouths of the two combatants in the divorce.

~

CHILDREN REMEMBER

Children may not divulge everything on their own, but they do have an unconscious inventory of all that goes on. They will remember down the road whether the procedure whereby the visiting parent came to take the child for their few hours or few days was a process that was filled with tension, or one that went smoothly. These children will talk to other children and compare notes. Undoubtedly, if the comparison shows that their parents made an extra effort to smooth the way for the children, those children will have a profound appreciation and escalating love for both the parents.

Should the custodial parent place obstacles in the way, or should the visiting parent be cantankerous, the child may fear saying anything confrontational to the offending parent. But the child will harbor ill-feelings that will spill over later on. What may seem at the moment to be a vindictive victory will later on boomerang into rejection of the parent by the child. It is simply not worth it.

~

THE GRANDPARENTS

There are other individuals who are involved in the ongoing post-divorce scenario. Probably the ones most affected, after the divorcing parents and children, are the grandparents. In the same way as father and mother do not cease to be father and mother after the divorce, the grandparents too do not cease to be grandparents after the divorce. And the grandparent connection is in force no matter what custodial arrangements have been incorporated.

The grandparents, for their part, should do all they can to maintain their relationship with the grandchild or grandchildren. They must make a transcending leap over the divorce situation, to assure that their link with the grandchildren is not severed.

They must resist the temptation to take sides in the issue of the divorce. Under normal circumstances one expects that the grandparents will take the side of their own child, and may harbor strong resentment for the child-in-law. However, it is wise for all grandparents to realize that just as marriage is a fifty-fifty proposition, so is divorce. With rare exception, the blame for the marriage not working out is not one-sided. Both of the marital partners are responsible. Blaming one or the other achieves nothing more than to further entrench bitterness.

~

TAKING THE LEAD

Once divorce has become inevitable, after all the appropriate steps to conserve the marriage have ended in failure, it is time to look forward rather than backward. Each of the grandparents is best advised to approach the child-in-law who may either have visitation privileges or custody, and assure them that they would like the relationship to continue, and to be free of animosity.

As the elders within the family, they have some responsibility to create the proper atmosphere. They can do so with this simple step. They should not assume that everything will be okay. Nor should they assume that any relationship that existed beforehand is doomed to non-existence. They should assume that whatever relationship will be ongoing in the future depends on the attitude that they take, and the approach that they bring to the situation. The custodial parent, as well as the visiting parent, should likewise realize that children under normal circumstances have a very warm relationship with the grandparents. Any attempt to deny the children such opportunities of grandparental love will backfire on the parents later on.

This denial may not be as serious as denying the child access to the other parent, but it is nevertheless serious. The grandparents are an inextricable part of the child's life, and can play an ongoing positive role. But whatever role they do play is dependent on the atmosphere created by the ones who most control the situation, namely the parents and the grandparents.

~

FAMILY INVOLVEMENT

The other members of the family, on either side, should likewise refrain from employing the convenient arguments that are of a partisan nature. Siblings, as a general rule, would like to come to the defense of a brother or sister who is going through a divorce.

When asked by strangers or friends what has happened, the initial defensive reaction is to speak about how one's brother or sister got entangled in a terrible marriage to an insensitive and callous marital partner. This type of comment will also be carried back, and eventually find its way to the other mate, with attendant negative consequences.

The family members are best off avoiding the blame syndrome. They should simply say that the marriage did not work out, but they hope that *the divorce will work out.*

~

THE DIVORCE WILL WORK OUT

This response may sound a trifle absurd to those questioners, who would like to hear some juicy gossip about an affair that took place within the marriage, or some really rambunctious fight between the couple, or some abuse of one of the partners by the other. It is most appropriate here to employ the ethical imperative to guard one's tongue, and to refrain from becoming involved in this most crude form of gossip-mongering.

The more people will resort to such comments as—"the marriage did not work out, but hopefully the divorce will work out amicably," the more such positive comments will become the norm.

It will become the norm, and the expected, that a divorcing couple maintains civility and respect for each other. With the divorce rate proliferating as it is, this is the only way one can avoid creating a situation of continual potential explosiveness within the community.

～

THE FRIENDSHIP NETWORK

One of the negative repercussions of divorce is that the old friendship networks may collapse. The divorcing couple may have had a close relationship with other couples during the marriage, but these relationships may suddenly disintegrate.

This may happen not because of animosity. It may be that others are in a quandary. They do not want to be caught in the middle, and feel that taking the side of one would be seen as betrayal by the other. So they do nothing, which quite often is the worst alternative.

The realization that because of the divorce you are not only losing a partner, but also an entire network of friends, can be devastating. This is when friends are desperately needed. To abandon in a time of need is to replace friendship with cruelty.

The Torah urges that when one's friend is slipping into poverty, that is the time to strengthen that person, to prevent the fall (Leviticus, 23:35). The couple who is divorcing is on a slipping, downhill course. If they are rejected by their former friends, they will indeed fall into spiritual impoverishment.

It is difficult to be single after divorce; it is difficult to be a single parent after divorce. Mothers are particularly vulnerable. Their economic situation suffers dramatically, and they are usually forced into the work force in order to manage. The break-up of the marriage leaves them lonely, sometimes also ashamed. If they handle the new reality successfully, they gain an enhanced sense of self-esteem. Former friends who remain friends can and must help in the transition. That is the ultimate expression of authentic caring, of unconditional friendship.

That friendship does not necessitate taking sides. It demands standing at the side of one's divorced friend, and helping by being an available ear, a calming influence, and a bedrock of emotional support.

~

PROJECTING AHEAD

All the parties involved in the divorce should project ahead to the Bar or Bat Mitzvah of the children, and their eventual marriage. They should think of what it will be like to be under one roof sharing a joyous event, but with such palpable animosity that the room is filled with tension, and subdivided into different factions. What should be a joyous event will then become an ordeal. The nature of that ordeal is such that it will generate more animosity, and more bitterness down the road.

No one wants to be locked into a life of misery. No responsible parent would want to inflict such misery upon children. Nor would any self-respecting parent want to deny the joys of grandparenthood to the grandparents. They would not, and therefore they should not.

Since the family is so central to Jewish continuity, divorce has implications for the Jewish community which extend beyond the immediate crisis. Divorce does create a rupture within the family, but that rupture need not become a permanent cleavage. With the proper attitude and the appropriate resolve, it is possible to retain some semblance of family after divorce. For the Jewish community, this is more than merely a possibility; it is a necessity.

———

THE OBVIOUS CHOICE

Whatever ensues in the post-divorce situation will probably be a reflection of how the divorcing couple actually behaves towards each other. If they behave with respect and goodwill toward each other, this will likely spill over into the attitude of the grandparents, and the extended family as well. If they are bitter towards each other, they will enlist the support of their family sides to justify their pettiness.

It is thus highly advisable that the divorcing couple resolves among themselves that they will put their best efforts into making the divorce as amicable as possible, and the post-divorce situation as manageable and respectful as possible. They should also resolve to transmit this desire to their own families, and to urge them to be kind and considerate to the other side of the family, to behave without acrimony or ill-will.

Once the syndrome of good will is set into motion, it will have ongoing positive reverberations. On the other hand, once the syndrome of bad will is initiated, it will have ongoing negative reverberations.

The choice of which button to push, and which road to take, is self-evident.

Chapter 14

RECONCILIATION — WITH FATE

FLAMES OF WRATH

When a marriage works well, a transcending blissfulness envelops the couple. When the marriage does not work, it can be an all-consuming fire. In the words of the Talmud, if the husband and wife are meritorious, their bliss is heavenly, with the Divine Presence abiding with them. If they are not meritorious, then they are engulfed in flames (Sotah, 17a).

The most fiery flames are the flames that threaten to devour the couple as they disentangle from their union. They are flames of anger and fury, outbursts of temper, charges and counter-charges, blame and counter-blame. Aside from the exceptional divorce which may take place in a relatively amicable atmosphere, the divorces which do have some rancor, and most do, are also full of hurt and trauma.

~

DEEP HURT

Each one of the couple would be less than normal if he or she did not feel a sense of hurt at what is transpiring. For each one, it is as if precious years have been thrown away. Added to that, the prospects for the future are uncertain. Each of the couple may be staring at a life of protracted loneliness. Particularly vulnerable is the woman who is left alone in her middle years, after the children have left the home. She will be considered too old to marry a younger person, and she herself will feel too young to marry an older person. She is caught in a bad bind, and feels betrayed by the turn of events that has left her all alone. It is entirely normal, and even to be expected, that a divorcing couple should go through a stage of agony, even despair, hurt, and anger. But there is life after divorce. It is important for the divorcing couple not only to honestly confront their feelings, but to also ask where these feelings will lead down the road.

~

EXTENDED UNHAPPINESS

A feeling of despair that lasts too long will become a depression. A feeling of anger which is protracted entrenches a bitterness that will adversely affect the rest of life, and as well the environment surrounding the embittered spouse. That environment includes the children, the grandparents, and the extended family. It is generally estimated that at the very least fifty people are immediately affected by a divorce. Anger spilling over to fifty people is a lot of ill-will. Multiply that by the thousands of divorces, perhaps close to 20,000 per year in the North American Jewish community, and that adds up to an unhappy community.

~

SELF-BLAME

When the decision to divorce is made by the couple in concert, as a mutual decision, there is less chance that bad feelings will develop. The ill-will is more likely to develop when one of the partners asks for a divorce from the other, to whom this request comes if not as a shock, at least as a terrible hurt. Often, the victimized partner will do some soul searching, afflicted by feelings of guilt at having been the cause of the breakdown in the marriage.

There may also be feelings of diminished self-esteem that arise from having been told to co-operate in a divorce. Instead of the marital partner asking—"where did we go wrong?," the question asked may be—"where did I go wrong?" The marital partner may feel anger at the mate who is launching the divorce action, and at the same time may harbor a feeling of dis-ease within the self for having failed. "How will I face my friends as a failure?" is the unspoken question asked.

~

HEALTHY CONTEMPLATION

It is easy, perhaps facile, to try to convince each of the marital partners that he or she was not to blame, that divorce is not proof of personal failure, or indicative of any inferiority. The couple needs time to assimilate the unfolding reality, even a certain amount of time for self-recrimination. After that, it is important for each of the marital partners to get on with life. Blaming the other or blaming the self for having failed in the marriage really achieves very little. What it does almost guarantee is that one's life will be focused on the past. One will continue to dredge up the past as a present quagmire from which extrication is next to impossible.

There is nothing wrong with looking at the past, as long as it is with a view towards the future. Thus, each of the marital partners who uses the experience of the failure in marriage to learn from it, to grow, and to approach life armed with this knowledge, will be able to face the future with renewed optimism.

~

PRAYING FOR THE EX

One of the more healthy exercises that a divorcing couple can engage in following the divorce is to pray for the welfare of their ex-marital partner. "One who prays for another individual and who is at the very same time in need will be answered first" (Talmud, Baba Kamma, 92a). Each of the marital partners who have now divorced needs nothing less than to find happiness and fulfillment in his or her life.

Often, the greatest obstacle to that happiness and fulfillment is the melancholic, dour mood that engulfs the divorced mate. Why not make a quantum leap in the opposite direction? What is wrong with each of the marital partners actually praying that their ex-mate finds the happiness in the future that was obviously not found in the past?

This type of prayer is a profound manifestation of the ability to conquer one's passions, to control one's anger, and to substitute good feelings and pleasant thoughts for ill-will. It is also a most effective way of avoiding the pro-

hibition, forbidding the pursuing of strife (Talmud, Sanhedrin, 110a). The post-divorce climate is most conducive to strife, and thus calls
for the marshalling of all inner resources to
resist that strife. By thinking in positive terms
rather than in negative terms, by praying for
the good of the other, the praying partner's
yearnings will almost immediately be
answered. The answer may not be in instantly
having found another partner in life; but at
least in having found inner tranquillity and
peace, through having rejected the all too
alluring temptation to be hateful and spiteful.

—

INTEGRATING

If it in fact turns out that the other partner did
succeed, and found a new marital partner, this
should then be translated into an ideal reason
to be truly happy for one's ex-mate. Each of
the ex-marital partners who has an expecta-
tion to remarry will undoubtedly want his or
her new marital partner to integrate well into
the family. They will be terribly upset, hurt,

and angry, if their former mate places obstacles in the path of the new marital partner. These obstacles can come in various forms, including being shut out from the home, being denied access, or with bad mouthing. Since neither of the partners would want this for himself or herself, they should not wish it on the other, or do anything to bring this about for the other.

The divorced partner who now has a new spouse should at the same time realize that whatever affection is shared with the new partner does not automatically transfer to the children. A mother who has found a new husband should not think that this new mate will displace the children's real father. He can and should love the children, but he is not a father substitute. Nor is the new wife of a divorced father to be perceived as a substitute mother.

For the new relationships to integrate well, they must avoid trespassing the entrenched boundaries of family function.

The rate of intermarriage for second marriages is astronomically high. Aside from this being fundamentally unacceptable, it creates tremendous difficulties for family integration, and is extremely unfair to the children. This is a multiple trespass which must be avoided.

~

EFFECTIVE BLENDING

The most effective way of preventing "blended family" pitfalls is by actually willing the best for the other, and rejoicing in the other's joy. By so doing, the chances that the other partner will reciprocate your happiness are increased.

This type of ethical behavior is fully consistent with, and a profound expression of the obligation to love the other as you love your own self. This means to avoid doing unto others that which is hateful to you, and instead wishing and doing for others what you would want from them.

A divorced couple who adheres to this ethical imperative will be well on the way to reconciling with their fate. The more and the better that each of the couple reconciles with his or her fate, the better they will be able to approach the future, and the more likely it is that they will have a fulfilling future.

Chapter 15

RECONCILIATION —
WITH MATE

~

UNFILLED EXPECTATIONS

Most couples who marry are reasonably
excited about what awaits them in the future.
They may not have fool-proof evidence, but
they share an inner feeling that the future
bodes well for them. They have high hopes
that marriage will bring them true love, contentedness, joy, and meaningful fulfillment.
Marriage, however, is complicated. With the
best of expectations, the rate of divorce that is
presently being experienced in society at large
indicates that often these expectations are not
met.

~

WHY IT FAILED

Why does the marriage fail to live up to expectations? This varies from couple to couple. Sometimes, the expectations are unrealistic. No matter how good the marital partner may be, he or she is human, not angelically perfect.

Sometimes, not enough attention is given to personality differences. The marriage may have been entered into with haste. In the eagerness to get married, the serious issue of compatibility was swept under the rug.

Or, it may be that extraneous factors impeded the development of a happy marital life. It could be that the couple's economic fortunes took a bad turn. They were not prepared to face the challenge of poverty, or even a life that is lived at less than the comfort level.

The difficulties may arise from unexpected interference from outside parties, be it parents-in-law or other family members, that has scraped away the tranquillity that the couple desired.

Or it could be an event, a traumatic event

within the family, that may have darkened the atmosphere, and the couple could not get back on track.

Or it could be that the marriage was not imbued with any real sense of values, and there was no meaningful sharing of the many family-strengthening events such as the *Shabbat*. The marriage drifts aimlessly into collapse.

~

BUILDING FOR THE FUTURE

All of these, plus a host of other possibilities, could help to explain why a relationship that was so full of promise went awry. The spouses have then drifted apart, and have even developed some animosity to, or alienation from one another. After all the interventions, they feel that they have no choice but to part company. They follow that feeling and part company.

The couple is now divorced from each other, and may have some ongoing communication, all the more likely if they did have children during the marriage.

After having come to grips with what has unfolded, and the failure of their relationship to live up to expectations, the couple, having reconciled with fate, will begin to rebuild their lives out of the wreckage of the failed marriage. The couple should reflect back on how it felt when things were going well, on the positive times experienced within the marriage, and when and how the marriage went astray.

There is much to be learned from what went wrong, so that the couple can be sure that the next time they will not repeat past mistakes.

~

LEARNING FROM EXPERIENCE

The rate of divorce for second marriages is greater than it is for first marriages. This means that, in general, the divorcing couple does not learn from their mistakes, and does not take divorce as seriously as they should.

A marital partner who is going through a second divorce will probably feel even more intense feelings of hurt, self doubt, diminished self-esteem, guilt, and possibly even despair. For it is now more than just one failed marriage. Now the person involved in the divorce is a two-time loser. There is a lingering stigma that is attached to anyone who is a two-time loser.

The statistics regarding second marriage failures should be a strong signal and message to couples who are divorcing, that they should try to learn much more about what went wrong the first time before contemplating a second attempt at marriage.

However, if each of the divorcing couple does actually try to glean the proper lessons from the failure of the first marriage, each can translate this awareness into a resolve. This is the resolve to be attentive to the pitfalls that can invade the marriage, to be alert to them and to handle them with care and with energy. The resolve not to make the same mistake a second time, and to do one's best to assure that the next marriage is a success, will almost but not quite guarantee that the second marriage will be better than the first.

～

WHY NOT

There is no rule which states that the second marriage must be to someone else. If the couple has actually gone through this serious investigatory process, and has come up with useful conclusions they feel will help them in the future, why not try to court the partner with whom you originally thought life would be so pleasing and fulfilling?

Granted, this is not always possible. Granted, there are divorces which are so filled with animosity that any talk of reconciliation following divorce is patently absurd. But aside from those situations when it is obvious that no amount of patchwork or repair can create a foundation for renewing the old acquaintance, there are other situations when there is not that much bad blood between the couple.

If the couple follows the positive track, starting simply, by adhering to the vital ethical

269

imperative not to cause affliction to the other, and escalating further to the more noble and higher ethic of doing that which is upright and good, thereby creating a pleasant atmosphere for conversation, why should the possibility of reconciliation with one's former mate be precluded?

There is so much talk about couples who drift apart after the early stages of marriage, to the point where they have "outgrown each other." If it is possible for couples to drift apart and away from one another, because of the different directions their lives take, is it not possible that the couple who grows via the divorce process can now once again find one another. If growing apart is possible, should not growing back together also be possible?

~

RECONCILING ON YOM KIPPUR

Yom Kippur is the day of universal reconciliation. For the entire community, *Yom Kippur*

(Day of Atonement) is the time for soul-searching, for investigating the failures of the past, and resolving to learn from those failures by not repeating them, and by embarking on a more positive track for the future. This is the essence of the repentance process.

This process can unfold only if the person who is repenting is honest with him- or herself, unabashed in the willingness to admit having made mistakes, and resolute and sincere in the commitment to betterment in the future. The person who behaves in such a manner is well on the way to reconciliation with God. The person has in effect re-entered under God's canopy, after having been distanced from it.

Sin, whether it be of commission or omission, causes a temporary divorce from one's Creator. The acknowledgment of the failing, and the resolve to correct it, bring about reconciliation with God. No one would dare suggest that since there has been an alienation from God, coming back again is impossible.

~

MODEL FOR DIVORCED COUPLES

It would be instructive to employ the *Yom Kippur* model for the divorced couple. The day on which the couple is married is looked upon as a *Yom Kippur*, when they start off with a clean slate. The couple can make for themselves a *Yom Kippur* following divorce, when each comes clean, and honestly comes to grips with the failings of the past.

Divorce, in its best case scenario, may be perceived as the darkness that comes between two marriages. But there is nothing which dictates that the first and the second mate cannot be one and the same person. If the couple has truly learned from their first mistakes, why not give the person who inspired that lesson the first chance at proving the lesson was well learned!

Chapter 16

JEWISH ETHICS
APPLIED TO DIVORCE

"Ethics of the Elders," what is popularly known as Pirkay Avot, contains timeless ethical instruction for all contingencies of life.

Since divorce is one of life's contingencies, it would be useful to extract from Ethics of the Elders appropriate ethical instruction that can be used as a guide in the divorce process.

What follows are some guidelines for a Jewish Divorce Ethic, consistent with the ideas presented in this volume, and which are suggested in Pirkay Avot.

~

Make for yourself a guide — Choose a person with wisdom and insight, to guide you through the difficult travail of the divorce process.

Keep far away from a bad neighbor — Do not let the undesirable behavior of your spouse influence you to behave in a like manner. Your behavior should be beyond reproach at all times.

Be of the disciples of Aharon, loving peace and pursuing peace — Obviously, loving peace and pursuing peace should help in keeping a marriage intact. However, even if the marriage has reached the point of being beyond repair, your love of peace and pursuit of peace should continue unabated, so that the divorce process is as tranquil as possible.

One who seeks a name loses one's name — If you enter into the divorce process trying to justify yourself, to maintain your honor, and to heap dishonor on your marital partner, you will lose your honor and your name.

If I am for my own self only, what am I? — If you are for yourself only, then this may be at

274

the root of the marriage's failure. However, do not carry that failure over into divorce. When divorcing, make sure that the welfare of others, including your spouse and children, are utmost in your mind.

Greet all people with a cheerful countenance — This across-the-board ethical imperative should include those people about whom you may not feel so cheery, including the mate that you are divorcing.

I have found nothing better for the body than silence — Especially when you hear insulting and degrading words from the former partner whom you have divorced, do not counter-attack and start a war. The best thing to do is to keep quiet. Maybe the verbal invective will disappear from the dialogue between you.

The world is preserved through three things: truth, justice, and peace — You should be able to accept the truth, the fact that after all has been attempted, the marriage is doomed to failure. As a next step, you should accept the verdict of the court, as it wades through the mass of details in order to hammer out a settlement of outstanding issues. And finally, having accepted the judgment, you should live with it, at peace with yourself, and committed to making the best of it for all others involved.

Which is the right path that a person should choose? That which is an honor to the one who does it and which also brings honor from humankind — If your behavior in the trying, traumatic process of divorce is ethically above board, it will enable you to look in the mirror with a clear conscience. It will also bring you the approbation of others, who will see your absolute commitment to uprightness even in the most trying times as a true model of what a human being should be.

Concentrate on three things and you will not fall into the grip of sin: Know what is above you — a seeing eye, a hearing ear, and all your deeds being recorded in a book — The this-worldly conflict of divorce may elicit, from the parties to the divorce, nastiness, ill-feeling, and the desire to exact revenge from the other. Were any of those contemplating such evil to be aware that others are listening in to their thoughts, and are aware of what they are plotting, they would be embarrassed.

They surely would think twice about carrying
this out. This is exactly the way the divorcing
couple should behave, knowing that God is
watching, that God is listening, and that God
is taking notes of all that is transpiring.

*Do not judge your fellow until you have
been in that person's position* — There may be
reasons why the marriage went sour, and you
may tend to blame the other partner for what
went wrong. However, you do not think the
way your partner thinks, nor do you feel the
same emotions that your partner feels. Quite
possibly, had you been in your partner's position, you would have reacted the same way as
your partner did, though you now blame your
partner for such behavior. By being cognizant
of this, you will avoid the blame trap.

*In a place where there are no people, strive
to be a person* — Even if you are hounded by a
spiteful ex-spouse who is mercilessly vindictive, who ridicules and reviles you, you should
be a mentsch at all times. Do not sink to that
level.

*Let your friend's honor be as dear to you as
your own* — Even in situations when you are
obviously hurt, and have a natural desire to

dishonor the mate whom you are divorcing, try to resist the temptation. You would not want to be dishonored in this already trying time.

Do not be easily provoked to anger — The process of divorce surely qualifies as an anger-evoking situation. You are angry at yourself, you are angry at your spouse, you are angry at the world. However, the more angry you get, the more angry you will be. You will not get rid of the anger; instead you will lock yourself into an anger pattern. The bitterness that is the outgrowth of this anger pattern will only make your life even more miserable. So, keep away from the anger.

A bad eye, bad passion, and hatred of one's fellow creatures drives a person out of the world — Your seeing the bad in the other, your having a bad passion, which in a divorce situation may be a passion to hate the person whom you once loved, and your ensuing hatred that emanates from this bad passion, drives you out of the world. You may think that by exercising your justified anger and hate you will ventilate, but in fact you will make yourself into less than a person. You will eventually drive

278

yourself out from meaningful existence. The hate will eat away at you.

Let your friend's possessions be as dear to you as your own — Do not enter into the divorce proceedings with the idea of making a killing, of taking as much out of your ex-marital partner as you can. Fairness and equity should prevail. You should be as caring and careful of your former spouse's possessions, as you would want that partner to be with your own, were you in that other person's position.

Let all your deeds be for the sake of Heaven — Make sure that whatever you do in the divorce process is for a higher purpose, namely to make the best out of the situation, and to assure the most harmonious post-divorce conditions possible. You do not have to answer to your friends, or your lawyer, or anyone else. Ultimately, you have to answer only to your Creator, so make sure that your actions are for Heaven's sake.

Do not consider yourself wicked — In the aftermath of divorce, you are likely to point the finger at yourself, and to feel guilty about what has transpired. Self-esteem can suffer in the process, and all hope for any future relationship diminishes. You can at one and the same time take responsibility for what occurred, and yet not consider yourself to be bad. Rather, consider yourself to be human, prone to error, but also able to learn from mistakes.

The day is short, the task is great, the workers are lazy, the reward is great, and the Master of the house is insistent — When divorce takes place, and the previously married couple lives apart, then that which came naturally now comes with difficulty. Previously short tasks are now enlarged, since each one of the divorced parents, whether custodial or visiting, now has a greater burden; one that must be shouldered alone. There may be a tendency to be daunted by the task at hand, but the reward for applying yourself to make the best of the situation is ample enough, and the master of the house, God, insists that you go through with it. It may be painful at first. The adjustment to new modes of communicating and meeting with your children, as prescribed by the custodial arrangement, may be complicated. But it must be done, and with resolve it will be done effectively.

One in whom the spirit of humankind takes delight, the spirit of the Omnipresent takes delight. But one in whom the spirit of humankind takes no delight, the spirit of the Omnipresent takes no delight — The ultimate Judge of the true worth of human behavior, God, judges based on how human beings react to the specific behavior. Since divorce and its aftermath are a time when an individual is most vulnerable, most likely to succumb to the easy enticement of launching a vendetta and behaving with spite, it is then that one's true character and one's inner nobility come to the fore. The behavior of the divorcing spouse which elicits the delight of humankind, who voice admiration for such restraint and good-will in a time of crisis, is one which God also notices. The reverse is also true. Unbecoming conduct, reducing oneself to base level behavior, will bring the condemnation of others, and likewise that of God.

If there is no proper conduct, there is no Torah — If, in the divorce situation, the couple behaves improperly, with no respect for one another, and resorting to all forms of devious speech and behavior to get their way, then this is an indication that however religious they may be, that religiosity is only perfunctory. They have not really grasped the essence of the Torah.

Who is wise? One who learns from all people — The wise person learns from all individuals and from all experiences. The wise person who is going through the agonizing throes of divorce will learn from that circumstance, will learn from the behaviors of those involved, and derive the right lessons on how to avoid such trauma in the future.

Who is mighty? One who conquers one's passions — The natural tendency, in divorce, is to desire to get back at the other partner for having caused all this grief. The strong person is the one who overcomes this desire, and instead behaves as a truly ethical and upright person.

Who is rich? One who rejoices in one's portion — Being satisfied, having basic needs taken care of, but not desiring to become overly wealthy at the expense of the other, will help facilitate the divorce settlement. Instead of trying to gouge the other, to fill one's own pockets, the thrust is just towards manageability. With such an attitude, the actual procedure of divorce will be more amicable. The individual who behaves with such a sense of self-satisfaction is likely to enhance the entire environment that is affected by the divorce.

Who is honored? One who honors humankind — The spouse who treats the other member of the divorcing couple with dignity and respect will likely have that respect reciprocated. Instead of a post-divorce situation characterized by ill-will and bitter recrimination, it will be characterized by respect and honor; truly a better alternative.

Do not despise any person — That includes a person whom you are most likely to despise, specifically the person whom you once loved.

Be of an exceedingly humble spirit, for the hope of the human being is decay — Instead of behaving with arrogance, trying to win points and pummel the other into submission in the divorce negotiations, behave with humility. In the end, all this bickering over material matters is of no lasting value. What really counts is that one behaved in a noble fashion. That is what endures forever.

Repentance and good deeds are as a shield against calamity — The spirit of wanting to better one's self, to correct the wrongs of the past and to embark on doing good deeds, in the aftermath of divorce, will avoid the calamity of bitterness, vindictiveness, and hatred associated with divorce.

When your enemy falls, do not rejoice — The person you may perceive to be your enemy, namely the spouse who has caused you so much agony through the divorce, is really not an enemy. But even if you perceive that spouse to be a foe, do not rejoice at the misfortune of your ex-mate. The ex-mate's misfortune will create a melancholic atmosphere that will spill over and eventually affect you too. Rather, you should hope that your ex-mate finds fulfillment and success.

Difficult to provoke and easy to pacify, this characterizes the pious person — This is the type of behavior pattern that is necessary to endure divorce and its aftermath.

Every controversy which is for the sake of Heaven will ultimately endure, but any con-

troversy which is not for the sake of Heaven will ultimately not endure — In the process of working out the arrangements following divorce, you may be involved in a fight for custody, honestly thinking that you are the better parent for your children. If this is an ego battle, then the children will not gain from it. However, if your intentions are genuine, purely for the children's welfare, then your concern for them as expressed in your argumentation will have lasting value. Its lasting value will be predicated on the fact that you present your view not out of bitterness, or through vilifying your ex-marital mate, but through the legitimacy of your position.

According the exertion is the reward — The extra effort that you expend in order to provide your children with the best in the difficult circumstances following divorce will bring its reward in that the children, through your encouragement and example, will be able to surmount the significant upheaval in their lives caused by the divorce.

Jewish ethics applied to divorce would go a long way towards lessening the trauma of divorce, and reducing the possibility that divorce develops into a no-holds-barred battle of perpetual duration. The ethical way is the better way for all involved, including the divorcing spouses, the larger family, and most importantly, the offspring.

Chapter 17
CONCLUDING THOUGHTS

~

SCARY PREDICTION

Divorce has become an accepted reality in today's society. Relatively recently, it was predicted that of every two marriages contracted in recent times, one would result in divorce. This was certainly not the original idea behind the famous observation that marriage is a fifty-fifty proposition. To think that there is a fifty-fifty chance that any marriage will "wind down" disintegrating is a scary thought for anyone contemplating marriage.

To make matters worse, a little while ago one respected observer of the Jewish scene predicted that the Jewish divorce rate would hit fifty percent of marriages contracted. There was no basis in reality for this prediction, save for the assumption that the trends in society eventually infiltrate the Jewish community.

~

HOPEFUL TREND

Thankfully, there has been a slight leveling of the trend, and the rate of divorce has not jumped, although this does not mean that the crisis within marriage has abated.

The crisis is real. The danger that marriage will not last is clear and present in literally every segment of Jewish society. No component of the community is immune, although assuredly the rate of divorce amongst the religious community is less than in the general community.

Again, to place matters in their true perspective, this does not mean that those marriages within the religious community are necessarily better marriages, or happier marriages. It may be that the stigma of divorce is still strong enough that the couple within the marriage endures, looks the other way, or tolerates what for many others would be an intolerable situation. So, whether the statistics for divorce are high or not, there is a crisis in the entire realm of marriage.

~

CRAZY QUESTION

Because divorce is a real possibility, it may be advisable for every individual, before contemplating marriage, to actually ask a crazy question. That crazy question is—"Is the mate whom I am marrying a mate whom I could divorce?" This question may seem absurd in the extreme, but before jumping to that conclusion, it is worthwhile contemplating what the question means.

Because marriages may not work, and instead will disintegrate, the question is whether the divorce will be a decent and civil one, or whether it will be a fight to the finish. It is wise to ask what type of mate you are taking. Are you taking the type of a mate who is nice and pleasant when the going is good, but who, whenever things do not go his or her way, reacts in a childish, spiteful, petty way?

If that is the case, then it is quite likely that such a mate will behave in a less than considerate way when it comes to divorce. Whoever it is that a person marries should be a person whom one would be able to divorce in a way which avoids recriminations, eschews protracted fighting, and eliminates perpetual conflict. In other words, the person whom you marry should be one who in your perception would be a mentsch, a true human being, even in the most trying circumstances.

Chances are that if an individual qualifies as one whom you could divorce with no fear of reprisal, he or she is the type of individual to whom you will be happily married, and the divorce will not be necessary. But it is important to ask the question, because by asking the question one may save much misery.

—

PERSONALITY FACTOR

Although there are many who place the blame for the rising rate of divorce on interactional problems within marriage, related to complications that impose themselves from the outside, there is a personal component to divorce which must be emphasized.

Marriage is the union of two individuals who, if they are of good character, should be able to live happily with each other. Invariably, in cases when marriage fails, one or both of the partners has a deficient personality. What is called marriage breakdown is really retarded personality development coming to the fore. That retarded development leads to a distorted set of values, including the inability to interact with people on a human level.

This statement, by the way, should not be seen as a contradiction of the earlier point made that the couple should not blame themselves for the marital failure to the point of despair and self-imposed melancholy. Often the very fact that there is a personality problem may not necessarily be the fault of the marital partner or partners, but is more directly related to their upbringing, and to the set of values which they adopted almost automatically from the culture in which they were raised.

This is important for the divorcing couple to realize. It is also vital to understand what is meant by the suggestion that a personality nuance may have been a contributing factor, or even the precipitating factor in the marriage breaking down. This is not to lay blame, but rather just to state facts, and to build upon the failure of the past towards the future.

A general observation about the divorce situation should not therefore translate into an imposition of guilt and despair upon the divorcing couple.

~

TRUE DIALOGUE

Huxley once said that "If individuality has no play, society does not advance: if individuality breaks out of all bounds, society perishes."

That same observation is true of human

development and of the marital sphere. It is best reflected in the famous words of Hillel, "If I am not for myself, who will be for me? And if I am for myself only, what am I . . . " (Talmud, Avot, 1:14). To be self-negating to the point of neglect of the self is irresponsible; but to be self-indulgent to the point of being oblivious to all others is to be irresponsive. The person who best relates to others is the one who has taken care of individual needs, who has a well developed sense of the self and of individual responsibility, as well as a realistic and honest appreciation of one's role in life.

This honest confrontation with one's self leads to a healthy outer directedness, to a concern with causes and for people. In short, the classic relationship between people demands an *I* to relate to a *thou*. But the real *I* will intentionally gravitate to a *thou*; not to fulfill a need, but to share the self. The true relationship with another person emanates from self-transcendence rather than from self-actualization.

~

TRANSCENDENCE IN MARRIAGE

Sharing of the self with another is, in the classical sense, expressed in marital union. Maimonides, in his Guide for the Perplexed (part 3, chapter 49), suggests that the female relatives whom a man may not marry share one common ingredient—namely that they are constantly together with him in the house, and arranging a marriage would be a relatively easy task. Maimonides also roundly condemns the union of root and branch, and sees this as one of the reasons behind the prohibition of consanguineous unions.

These two factors, the constant togetherness and the root-branch idea, point to a vital ingredient in any marriage. The respective spouses are obliged to marry people who are in some sense strangers, people who can be called other. Confining one's self to one's own immediate environment is seen as abhorrent.

This abhorrence stems from the reality that such a union involves not an extension of the self, but instead a turning in of the self, a shrivelling up, a recoiling into a comfortable shell. It is an exercise in self-centeredness, and is the very antithesis of healthy human interaction, and hence of good marriage.

~

THE RIGHT FOCUS

Self-centeredness as manifested in the form of hyper-reflection on the self is considered to be the prime cause of impotence and frigidity between couples. Whether it stems from a strong desire to be able to perform, or an excessive drive for self-satisfaction, it causes increasing difficulty and frustration. Eventually, it results in the inability to communicate sexually with the partner.

The best means of attaining the pleasure of marital union is by not intending it, but instead by letting it flow as the natural outgrowth of a true love relationship. Happiness, instead of being pursued, should ensue.

It is worthwhile to use the sexual model as paradigmatic for marriage itself. Sex is the language of marriage; it is marriage's distinct form of communication. The problem of hyper-reflection on the self which causes breakdowns in sexual communication is also at work in verbal communication. This is not to say that when there are problems of a sexual nature the marriage is a failure, but the symptomatology is quite the same.

Not surprisingly, the subservience to the ethic of self-realization has been implicated as a significant factor in the increasing number of divorces. Paradoxically, when each partner is primarily concerned not with the self but with the other person, both the functional and the spiritual aspects of the union are significantly enhanced. Thus, the concept of extending the self toward the other is a philosophical and functional truth. All communication works better when the focus is on trying to understand the other, and being committed to bringing out the best in the other.

MATURITY

The self which extends toward the other in the marital context should be a mature self. The mature self has, through growth and commitment, assumed responsibility for personal welfare. In the words of the Talmud, " . . . A man should build a house, plant a vineyard, and then marry a woman" (Sotah, 44a,). Maimonides, in an extraordinary vignette, states that "It is the way of fools first to marry and then build a house and find a profession" (Mishnah Torah, Hilkhot De'ot, 5:11).

Before a person has established inner stability and peace — symbolized by the building of a home, and before having planted a vineyard (i.e., before having placed the self on a firm financial footing, so that one's primary personal needs have been met), it is premature, even foolish to marry. When the marriage itself is expected to create the financial and emotional stability that are so vital, but missing prior to marriage, the marriage is in trouble from the outset.

Marriage is ideally the union of two complete people, who unite not to fulfill personal needs or satisfy drives, but to exercise mutual growth through reciprocal concern for each other. The purpose in marriage is not to *get*, but to give. How ironic it is that those who do not focus on giving will end up "*getting!*" But getting a *get* is something they could do without.

～

SHARING

The ideal of immersion in the other can hardly be realized when each, or even one, still has unresolved problems or basic character deficiencies. In such cases the wedlock is not one of true love, but instead an alliance for need gratification. It is a caused and dependent relationship, rather than a spontaneous and independent one. Eventually, "All love that depends on a cause will pass away once the cause is no longer there, but that love which is not dependent on a cause will never pass away" (Avot, 5:16). The marriage may survive, but it will not thrive.

It is stated that "Any man who has no wife is no proper man" (Talmud, Yevamot, 63a). This is not to imply that a man should marry at any cost. This statement simply asserts that reaching a pronounced level of maturity and self-sufficiency is only the first step in human endeavor.

The next step is to extend that mature self toward another. The person who thinks that manhood is achieved through being independent and aloof is, in the words of the Talmud, no proper man. For, in all instances, true maturity is perceived through interaction with others, not through wallowing in self-indulgence. The inability to share, to give of one's self, whether it stems from immaturity, or from the character deficiency most easily described as self-centeredness, is usually at work in marriage breakdown. It is a personality flaw coming to the fore, with sometimes tragic consequences.

~

NO CONTENTEDNESS

A match between spouses is known as a *shidukh*. Rabbi Moshe Isserles identifies this with the word for contentedness, menuhah (Shulhan Arukh, Yoreh De'ah, 228:43). No one can today be content with the uneasy state in which many *shidukhim* (matches) find themselves. Yet Jews throughout history have been able to react positively to crisis. On countless occasions they have been able to transmute potential tragedy into human triumph. If Jews can today restore the ingredient of contentedness to the marital sphere, it will rank as a singular achievement of the will.

If we can address the proliferating number of divorces with forthrightness and dedication, we can perhaps rescue some form of functionality from the tentacles of disaster. Otherwise we will have a community in which so many are at war with each other. This is not the stuff upon which a solid posterity is built. Divorce, as an issue confronting the Jewish community, must be tackled at both ends. At the front end, a priority must be placed on empathy, on understanding, on sharing, and on giving, so that one will not have to *get*. At the tail end, acknowledging that there will be divorces within the community — that this is inevitable — the community in its entirety, leadership in all spheres, must insist on the implementation of Jewish divorce ethics.

~

ENTER GOD

Peace is so vital to the community that, in the words of the Midrash (Leviticus Rabbah, 9:9), "God allows the Name of God to be erased into water, to effect harmony between husband and wife." Such erasure is a serious sacrilege, but when it is done in the ritual of reconciliation, it is permitted, even mandated.

When the peacefulness of the couple is upset, and divorce finalized, God's Name is erased. There is little vestige of Godliness, of a higher code of ethics, in the behavior of many couples going through the process of divorce. But God, and the transcending ethic that emanates from God, must be as much a part of divorce as of marriage.

The problem is obvious, the need for action is imperative. If not now, when? (Avot, 1:14). Acting with immediacy in the face of a crisis is itself an ethical imperative.

BIBLIOGRAPHY

Appleton, Jane, and William Appleton. *How not to Split Up*. New York: Berkley Books, 1979.

Azikri, R. Eliezer. *Sefer Haredim*. Jerusalem, 1972.

Belli, Melvin & Mel Krantzler. *The Complete Guide for Men and Women Divorcing*. New York: St. Martins Press, 1988.

Berger, Stuart. *Divorce Without Victims: Helping Children Through Divorce With a Minimum of Pain and Trauma*. New York: New American Library, 1983.

Bleich, J. David. A Suggested Antenuptial Agreement: A Proposal in Wake of Avitzur. *Journal of Halacha and Contemporary Society*, Spring 1984, 7, 25–41.

Blood, Bob, and Margaret Blood. *Marriage*. New York: Free Press, 1978.

Blumstein, Philip, and Pepper Schwartz.

American Couples: Money, Work, Sex. New York: William Morrow, 1983.

Breaking the Divorce Cycle. *Newsweek*, January 13, 1992, 48–53.

Bulka, Reuven P. The Role of the Individual in Jewish Law. *Tradition: A Journal of Orthodox Jewish Thought*, Spring-Summer 1973, 13 (14) – 14 (1), 124–136.

Bulka, Reuven P. Divorce: The Problem and the Challenge. *Tradition: A Journal of Orthodox Jewish Thought*. Summer 1976, 16 (1), 127–133.

Bulka, Reuven P. Honesty vs. Hypocrisy. *Judaism*, Spring 1976, 23(2), 209–216.

Bulka, Reuven P. Philosophical Foundations for Marriage Counseling. In Joseph Fabry, Reuven Bulka, and William Sahakian (Eds.), *Logotherapy in Action*. New York: Jason Aronson, 1979, 138–145.

Bulka, Reuven P. *As a Tree by the Waters — Pirkey Avoth: Psychological and Philosophical Insights*. New York: Philipp Feldheim, 1980.

Bulka, Reuven P. Some Implications of Jewish Marriage Philosophy for Marital Breakdown. *Pastoral Psychology*, Winter 1981, 30(2), 103–112.

Bulka, Reuven P. Love Your Neighbor: Halakhic Parameters. *Journal of Halacha and Contemporary Society*, Fall 1988, 16, 43–54.

Chigier, Moshe. *Husband and Wife in Jewish Law*. Jerusalem: Harry Fischel Institute, 1985.

Davids, Leo. Jewish Marriage Breakdown in Canada: Some Plain Facts. *Rabbinical Council of America Family and Marriage Newsletter*, Winter 1981, 5 (2), 1–4.

Don-Yechiya, Benny. *Mishpahah B'Mishpat: Madrikh L'Dinay Ishut*. Tel Aviv: Hok U'Mishpat, 1983.

Epstein, Mendel. *A Woman's Guide to the Get Process*. Israel: Private Printing, 1989.

Epstein, R. Yehiel. *Arukh haShulhan* (8 vols.). New York: Grossman Publishing House, no date.

Epstein, Yosef. *Mitzvat HaShalom*. New York: Torat Ha'Adam Institute, 1969.

Epstein, Yosef. *Sefer Mitzvot HaBayit*. New York: Torat Ha'Adam Institute, 1975.

Falk, Zev. *Dinay Nisuin*. Jerusalem: Mesharim, 1983.

Fertel, Norman and Esther Feuer. Treating Marital and Sexual Problems in the Orthodox Jewish Community. *Journal of Psychology and Judaism*, Spring-Summer 1981, 5 (2), 85–94.

Fried, Jacob. *Jews and Divorce*. New York: Ktav Publishing House, 1968.

Gardner, Richard. *The Boys and Girls Book about Divorce: With an Introduction for Parents*. New York: Bantam Books, 1971.

Gartner, Tzvi. Problems of a Forced Get. *Journal of Halacha and Contemporary Society*, Spring 1985, 9, 118–142.

Gibson, Nancy. *Separation and Divorce: A Canadian Woman's Survival Guide*. Edmonton, Alberta: Hurtig Publishers, 1986.

Glick, Paul and Arthur Norton. Marrying, Divorcing and Living Together in the U.S. Today. *Population Bulletin*, October 1977, 32 (5), 36–37.

Goldstein, Sol. *Divorced Parenting: How to Make it Work*. Toronto: McGraw-Hill Ryerson, 1982.

Gottleib, Dorothy Weiss, Inez Bellow Gottleib, & Marjorie A. Slavin. *What to Do When Your Son or Daughter Divorces*. New York: Bantam Books, 1988.

Gottman, John, Cliff Notarius, Jonni Gonso, and Howard Markham. *A Couple's Guide to Communication*. Champaign, Ill.: Research Press, 1976.

Grollman, Earl. *Talking About Divorce and Separation*. Boston: Beacon Press, 1975.

Haut, Irwin H. *Divorce in Jewish Law and Life*. New York: Sepher-Hermon Press, 1983.

Herring, Basil F. *Jewish Ethics and Halakhah for Our Time* (Volume 2). Hoboken, New Jersey: Ktav Publishing House & New York: Yeshiva University Press, 1989.

Hootman, Marcia, & Patt Perkins. *How to Forgive your Ex-Husband and Get on with Your Life*. New York: Warner Books, 1985.

Jakobovits, Immanuel. Marriage and Divorce. In Leo Jung (Ed.), *Woman*, (Vol. 3 of *The Jewish Library*). London: Soncino Press, 1970, 101–121.

Jerusalem Talmud (5 vols.). New York: Otzar HaSefarim, 1968.

Karo, R. Yosef. *Shulhan Arukh* (10 vols.). New York: M.P. Press, 1965.

Klagsbrun, Francine. *Married People: Staying Together in the Age of Divorce*. New York: Bantam Books, 1985.

Kranzler, Gershon. The Changing Orthodox Jewish Family. *Jewish Life*, Summer-Fall 1978, 23–36.

Krauss, Simcha. Litigation in Secular Courts. *Journal of Halacha and Contemporary Society*, Spring 1982, 2 (1),35–53.

Lansky, Vicki. *Divorce Book for Parents: Helping Your Children Cope with Divorce and its Aftermath*. New York: New American Library, 1989.

Levinger, George, & Oliver Moles (Eds.). *Divorce and Separation: Context, Causes, and Consequences*. New York: Basic Books, 1979.

Maimonides, R. Moses. *Mishnah Torah* (6 vols.). New York: M.P. Press, 1962.

Maimonides, R. Moses. *The Guide for the Perplexed*. London: Dover Publications, 1931.

Matthews, Arlene. *Why Did I Marry You, Anyway?* New York: Pocket Books, 1988.

Medved, Diane. *The Case Against Divorce.* New York: Donald I. Fine, Inc., 1989.

The Midrash (10 vols.). H. Freedman & M. Simon (Eds.). London: Soncino Press, 1961.

Mikraot Gedolot (Holy Scriptures and Commentaries)(10 vols.). New York: Pardes Publishing House, 1951.

Piskay Din Shel Batay Hadin Harabaniyim B'Yisrael (12 vols.). Jerusalem: Weiss Printing & Ministry of Religion.

Poretz, Mel & Barry Sinrod. *The First Really Important Survey of American Habits.* Los Angeles: Price Stern Sloan, Inc., 1989.

Rofes, Eric (Ed.). *The Kids' Book of Divorce: By, For, and About Kids.* New York: Vintage Books, 1982.

Savells, Jerald & Lawrence J. Cross (Eds.). *The Changing Family: Making Way for Tomorrow.* New York: Holt, Rinehart, and Winston, 1978.

Schaffer, Sylvan. Child Custody: Halacha and the Secular Approach. *Journal of Halacha and Contemporary Society,* Fall 1983, 6, 33–45.

Schlesinger, Benjamin. Reflections on Family

Breakdown Among Jewish Families. *Journal of Psychology and Judaism*, Fall 1976, 1(1), 45–53.

Schwartz, Gedalia. Heter Meah Rabbanim. *Journal of Halacha and Contemporary Society*, Spring 1986, 11, 33–49.

Shapiro, Daniel Z. *Thinking Divorce? Consider the Shocking Personal and Financial Realities*. Binghamton, New York: Almar Press, 1983.

Shereshevsky, Ben Zion. *Dinay Mishpahah*. Jerusalem: Reuven Mass, 1989.

The Talmud (19 vols.). New York: M.P. Press, 1965.

Tavris, Carol. *Anger: The Misunderstood Emotion*. New York: Simon & Schuster, 1984.

Trafford, Abigail. *Crazy Time: Surviving Divorce*. New York: Bantam Books, 1984.

Van Buren, Abigail. *The Best of Dear Abby*. New York: Pocket Books, 1981.

Vaughan, Diane. *Uncoupling: How Relationships Come Apart*. New York: Vintage Books, 1987.

Wallerstein, Judith & Joan Kelly. *Surviving the Breakup: How Children and Parents*

Cope with Divorce. New York: Basic Books, 1980.

Wallerstein, Judith S. & Sandra Blakeslee. *Second Chances: Men, Women, and Children a Decade after Divorce.* New York: Ticknor & Fields, 1989.

Warburg, Ronald. Child Custody: A Comparative Analysis. *Israel Law Review*, October 1979, 14 (4), 480–503.

Waxman, Chaim. The Threadbare Canopy: The Vicissitudes of the Jewish Family in Modern American Society. *American Behavioral Scientist*, March-April 1989, 23 (4), 467–486.

Waxman, Chaim I. *America's Jews in Transition.* Philadelphia: Temple University Press, 1983.

Weinberger, Bernard. The Growing Rate of Divorce in Orthodox Jewish Life. *Jewish Life*, Spring 1976, 9–14.

Weiss, Robert. *Marital Separation.* New York: Basic Books, 1975.

Weiss, Robert. *Going it Alone: The Family Life and Social Situation of the Single Parent.* New York: Basic Books, 1979.

Yankelovich, Daniel. *New Rules: Searching*

*for Self-Fulfillment in a World Turned
Upside Down*. New York: Bantam Books,
1982.

GLOSSARY

agunah — literally, tied down, anchored. Refers to woman unable to marry because she has no religious divorce (get).

Bet Din — Rabbinical Court.

get — Jewish religious divorce.

Gittin — Talmudic Tractate dealing mainly with divorce; alternately, the plural for get.

golah — outside Israel.

hakarat hatov — recognizing and appreciating the good done for you by others.

halakhah — Jewish law applied to life.

halakhic — pertaining to halakhah (Jewish law).

Havdalah — separating prayer-blessing, signaling end of Sabbath or festival.

heter — permission.

ketubah — marriage contract.

Kiddush — sanctification prayer-blessing ushering in the Sabbath or festival.

Kiddushin — Talmudic tractate dealing

mainly with marriage; alternately, sanctification toward marriage, i.e., betrothal.

kohen — member of the priestly family.

mentsch — genuine human being, of high ethical and moral stature.

menuhah — contentedness.

Midrash — Rabbinic exegesis in the form of homily.

mikvah — ritual bath used for immersion in certain situations.

mitzvah — commandment.

mored — rebellious husband.

moredet — rebellious wife.

Nisuin — marriage.

onah — literally, her time; refers to conjugal obligations.

ptur — documented proof of religious divorce.

Rabbenu Gershom — 12th century sage who enacted regulations forbidding a man having more than one wife at a time, and also preventing a husband from divorcing his wife against her will.

Sephardi — descendants of Jews who lived in Spain or Portugal prior to the expulsion of 1492.

Shabbat — seventh day of the week, celebrated as a day of cessation from material creativity with the purpose of generating spiritual reinvigoration, from Friday before sundown to Saturday after sunset.

shehitah — specific religious procedure, pain-free and quick, to prepare animal or fowl for eating.

shidukh — match of a couple for marriage.

shidukhim — plural of shidukh.

sofer — scribe, expert in writing scrolls or bills of divorce.

Talmud — Tractates containing explication of the Torah by the Rabbinic sages.

Torah — The revealed instruction on life transmitted by God to the people of Israel.

Yom Kippur — Day of Atonement.

Yom Tov — Sacred Festival in Jewish calendar of celebrations, including Pesah, Shavuot, and Sukkot.

zuz — coin.

BOOKS BY THE AUTHOR

The Wit and Wisdom of the Talmud. Mt. Vernon, New York: Peter Pauper Press, 1974. (Second Printing, 1983).

Logotherapy in Action. Co-Editor with Joseph Fabry and William Sahakian. New York: Jason Aronson, 1979.

Mystics and Medics: A Comparison of Mystical and Psychotherapeutic Encounters (Ed.). New York: Human Sciences Press, 1979.

Sex and the Talmud: Reflections on Human Relations. Mt. Vernon, New York: Peter Pauper Press, 1979.

The Quest for Ultimate Meaning: Principles and Applications of Logotherapy. New York: Philosophical Library, 1979.

As a Tree by the Waters — Pirkey Avoth: Psychological and Philosophical Insights. New York: Feldheim, 1980.

Holocaust Aftermath: Continuing Impact on the Generations (Ed.). New York: Human Sciences Press, 1981.

A Psychology-Judaism Reader. With Moshe HaLevi Spero as Co-Editor. Springfield, Illinois: Charles C. Thomas, 1982.

Dimensions of North American Orthodox Judaism (Ed.). New York: Ktav Publishing Company, 1983.

Torah Therapy: Reflections on the Weekly Sedra and Special Occasions. New York: Ktav Publishing Company, 1983. (Second Printing, 1990).

The Coming Cataclysm: The Orthodox-Reform Rift and the Future of the Jewish People. Oakville, Ontario: Mosaic Press, 1984. (Second Edition, 1986).

Loneliness. Toronto: Guidance Centre of the University of Toronto, 1984.

The Haggadah for Pesah: With Translation and Thematic Commentary. Jerusalem: Pri Haaretz Publications, 1985.

Jewish Marriage: A Halakhic Ethic. Hoboken, New Jersey: Ktav Publishing Company, 1986. (Second Printing, 1991).

The Jewish Pleasure Principle. New York: Human Sciences Press, 1986. (Paperback Edition, 1989).

Individual, Family, Community: Judeo-

Psychological Perspectives. Oakville, Ontario: Mosaic Press, 1989.

What You Thought You Knew About Judaism: 341 Common Misconceptions about Jewish Life. Northvale, New Jersey: Jason Aronson, 1989. (Second Printing, 1991).

Uncommon Sense for Common Problems. Toronto: Lugus Productions, 1990.

Critical Psychological Issues: Judaic Perspectives. Lanham, Maryland: University Press of America, 1992.